common core

(3) # Performance Coach

Mathematics

Performance Coach, Mathematics, Grade 3   310NASE   ISBN-13: 978-1-62362-805-5
Cover Illustration: © Thinkstock

Triumph Learning® 136 Madison Avenue, 7th Floor, New York, NY 10016

CONTENTS

DEAR STUDENT

Welcome to *Performance Coach*!

We made this book to help you strengthen your mathematics skills. These skills are important to have for every subject you study this year, not just Mathematics.

Each lesson in this book has three parts:

GETTING THE IDEA ①

Review some of the basic concepts and skills you've already learned.

② COACHED EXAMPLE

Solve a problem. There are several questions that will help you along the way!

LESSON PRACTICE ③

Now you're on your own! This part contains more problems to solve.

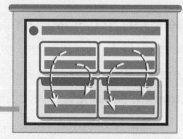

There are many different types of test items in *Performance Coach*. For some, you will have to choose more than one answer. For others, you will write out your answer. You will also see items that ask you to complete a graph, table, or sentence. Many items have more than one part. Be sure to read the directions carefully so you know how to answer each item.

HAVE A GREAT YEAR!

Sincerely,
TRIUMPH LEARNING

DOMAIN 1

Operations and Algebraic Thinking

Introducing Multiplication

Equal groups are groups that have the same number of objects.

Each group has 4 dogs. There are 3 equal groups.

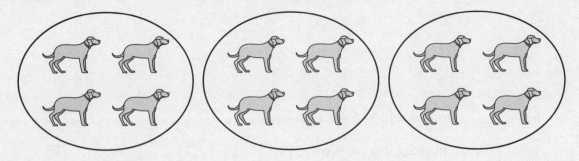

When you combine equal groups, you can add to find the total number of objects.

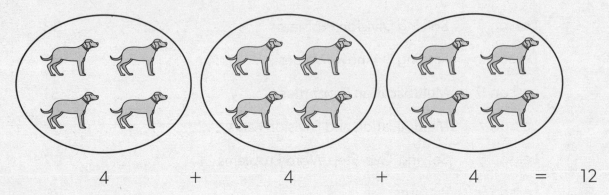

4   +   4   +   4   =   12

There are 12 dogs in all.

You can also use **multiplication** to find the total number of objects in equal groups. The numbers you multiply are **factors**. The answer is the **product**. Write a multiplication number sentence.

3 groups of 4 dogs each is 12 dogs in all.

$$3 \quad \times \quad 4 \quad = \quad 12$$

$$\uparrow \qquad \uparrow \qquad\qquad \uparrow$$

factors   product

Another way to show multiplication is to make an array. An **array** is a set of objects arranged in equal rows. An array for 3 × 4 = 12 has 3 rows, and each row has 4 objects.

Example 1

Find the product.

4 × 7 = ☐

Strategy   Make an array.

Step 1   What can 4 × 7 mean?

4 × 7 can mean 4 equal groups of 7 objects each.

It can also mean 4 rows of 7 objects each.

Step 2   Make an array.

Step 3   Find the total number of objects in the array.

4 rows of 7 counters each is 28 counters in all.

4   ×   7   =   28

factors   product

Solution   4 × 7 = 28

You can use an area model to help you with multiplication.

An **area model** is a rectangle made of square tiles. It is similar to an array.

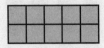

2 rows of 5 square tiles each is 10 square tiles in all.

$$2 \quad \times \quad 5 \quad = \quad 10$$

factors   product

Example 2

Find the product.

$$5 \times 6 = \square$$

Strategy   **Make an area model.**

Step 1   Use grid paper to draw an area model.

Draw a rectangle with 5 rows of 6 square tiles each.

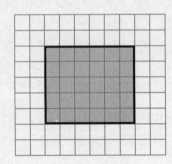

Step 2   Find the total number of square tiles.

5 rows of 6 square tiles each is 30 square tiles in all.

Solution $5 \times 6 = 30$

You can also multiply to find the total when combining equal measurements, such as equal lengths or equal weights.

Example 3

Maria has 3 pieces of ribbon. Each piece of ribbon is 2 feet long. Write a number sentence to show how many total feet of ribbon Maria has.

Strategy **Make a diagram of the problem.**

Step 1 Draw a diagram of the pieces of ribbon Maria has.

2 feet	2 feet	2 feet

Step 2 Determine what operation you can use.

There are 3 pieces of ribbon. Each ribbon is the same length.

To find the total length of the ribbon, multiply.

Step 3 Write a number sentence.

3 pieces of ribbon each 2 feet long is 6 feet of ribbon in all.

$3 \times 2 = 6$

Solution **The number sentence $3 \times 2 = 6$ shows that Maria has a total of 6 feet of ribbon.**

Example 4

Use the multiplication sentence $5 \times 9 = 45$ to describe a situation.

Strategy **Use the definition of multiplication.**

Step 1 Identify the meaning of $5 \times 9 = 45$.

5 and 9 are factors. They can mean 5 groups of 9 objects.

45 is the product. It can mean there are 45 objects in all.

Step 2 Think of a real-world situation.

There are 5 baseball teams with 9 players on each team.

There are 45 players in all.

Solution **The sentence $5 \times 9 = 45$ can describe the total number of players on 5 baseball teams, each with 9 players.**

Lila made 2 fruit baskets. She will give them as gifts. The fruit in each basket is shown.

Basket A	Basket B
4 bananas	4 bananas
5 apples	4 apples
3 pears	4 pears

Lila wants to find the total number of pieces of fruit in each basket. For which basket can Lila write a multiplication sentence?

Use multiplication to find the total number of objects in groups that have _____ number of objects.

In Basket A, there are _____ kinds of fruit.

The number of each kind of fruit is _____.

Can you write a multiplication sentence? _____

In Basket B, there are _____ kinds of fruit.

The number of each kind of fruit is _____.

Can you write a multiplication sentence? _____

So, Lila can multiply to find the total number of pieces of fruit in Basket _____.

She can write the multiplication sentence _____.

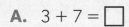 **LESSON PRACTICE**

1 Draw a line from each number sentence to the model that represents it.

A. $3 + 7 = \square$ •

B. $3 \times 7 = \square$ •

C. $7 + 6 + 7 = \square$ •

  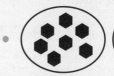

2 Draw an area model for the multiplication problem below. Then find the product.

$7 \times 3 =$ _____

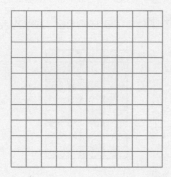

3 Which number sentence tells how many counters are in the array? Mark all that apply.

○ **A.** $6 + 3 = 9$

○ **B.** $3 \times 6 = 18$

○ **C.** $3 + 3 = 6$

○ **D.** $6 \times 3 = 18$

○ **E.** $6 + 6 + 6 = 18$

4 The number sentence describes the array below. Circle numbers to make the number sentence true.

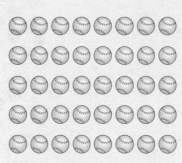

$$5 \times \begin{array}{|c|} \hline 5 \\ \hline 8 \\ \hline 40 \\ \hline \end{array} = \begin{array}{|c|} \hline 5 \\ \hline 8 \\ \hline 40 \\ \hline \end{array}$$

5 Read each statement about the area model below. Select True or False.

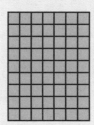

A. You can add 7 nine times to find the total number of tiles in the area model.　　○ True　○ False

B. The sum of 9 + 7 + 9 + 7 tells how many square tiles are in the area model.　　○ True　○ False

C. You can multiply the factors 9 and 7 to find the total number of tiles.　　○ True　○ False

D. The product of 9 × 7 tells how many square tiles are in the area model.　　○ True　○ False

E. The area model shows the product is 54.　　○ True　○ False

6 Which model represents 4 × 5? Mark all that apply.

○ A.

○ B.

○ C.

○ D.

○ E.

      4 inches   4 inches   4 inches   4 inches

7 Look at the number sentence.

$7 \times 5 = 35$

Use the multiplication sentence to describe a situation.

8 Decide if you can use multiplication to solve each problem. Select Yes or No.

A. A model train has 8 cars. Each car is 6 inches long. How long is the train? ○ Yes ○ No

B. Max had 5 shells. He found 7 more shells. How many shells does Max have in all? ○ Yes ○ No

C. An area model has 8 square tiles. Another area model has 6 square tiles. How many square tiles are in both area models? ○ Yes ○ No

D. There are 7 birds in each of 5 trees. How many birds are in all of the trees? ○ Yes ○ No

9 Ben has 24 flowers to plant. He wants to plant them in equal rows.

Part A

Show 3 different ways that Ben could plant the flowers. Draw an array to show each way.

Part B

Write a multiplication sentence to represent each way.

Introducing Division

1 GETTING THE IDEA

Division can be used to find the number of objects in equal groups.

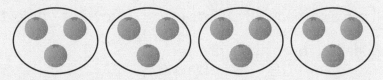

When 12 oranges are divided into 4 equal groups, there are 3 oranges in each group.

The result of a division problem is the **quotient**. Write a number sentence.

$12 \div 4 = 3$

↑

quotient

You can also use division to find the number of equal groups when sharing objects.

When 12 oranges are divided into groups of 3 oranges each, there are 4 equal groups.

$12 \div 3 = 4$

Another way to show division is to make an **array**.

An array for $32 \div 4 = 8$ has 4 objects in each row.

It has 8 equal rows.

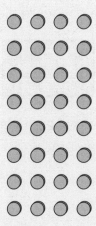

Example 1

Find the quotient.

$$28 \div 7 = \square$$

Strategy   Make an array.

Step 1   What can $28 \div 7$ mean?

       $28 \div 7$ can mean 28 objects divided into groups of 7 objects each.

       It can also mean 28 objects placed in rows of 7 objects each.

Step 2   Draw the first row of the array.

Step 3   Continue to draw equal rows in the array until there are 28 counters in all.

Step 4   Find the number of rows in the array.

       When 28 counters are divided into rows of 7 counters, there are 4 rows.

       $28 \div 7 = 4$

Solution $28 \div 7 = 4$

Remember that an **area model** made of square tiles is similar to an array.

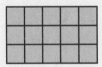

Suppose you know the total number of square tiles and the number of square tiles in each row. You can divide to find the number of rows.

Example 2

Tony is using 8 square tiles to make a design. He will place 4 square tiles in each row. How many rows will Tony make? Find the quotient.

$$8 \div 4 = \square$$

Strategy   Make an area model.

Step 1   Shade 1 row of 4 square tiles.

Step 2   Draw equal rows until there are a total of 8 square tiles.

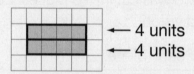

← 4 units
← 4 units

Step 3   Count the number of rows that were made.

An area model with a total of 8 square tiles and 4 square tiles in each row has 2 rows. The quotient is 2.

Solution   Tony will make 2 rows of square tiles. $8 \div 4 = 2$.

You can also divide to solve measurement problems.

Example 3

Tarik had a board that was 16 feet long. He cut it into 8 equal pieces. Write a number sentence that shows how many feet long each piece is.

Strategy   **Make a diagram of the problem.**

Step 1   Draw a diagram of the board Tarik cut. Model each foot.

| 1 ft | 1 ft | 1 ft | 1 ft | 1 ft | 1 ft | 1 ft | 1 ft | 1 ft | 1 ft | 1 ft | 1 ft | 1 ft | 1 ft | 1 ft | 1 ft |

Step 2   Determine what operation you can use.

A 16-foot board was cut into 8 pieces. Each piece is the same length. You can use division.

Step 3   Find the length of each piece.

Make 8 equal pieces. Each piece is 2 feet long.

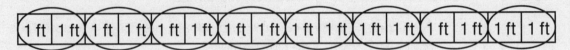

Step 4   Write a number sentence.

$16 \div 8 = 2$

Solution   **The number sentence $16 \div 8 = 2$ shows that each piece is 2 feet long.**

Example 4

Use the division sentence 35 ÷ 5 = 7 to describe a situation.

Strategy   Use the definition of division.

Step 1   Identify the meaning of 35 ÷ 5 = 7.

35 is the total number of objects.
5 could be the number of objects in each group.
7 is the quotient. It could be the number of groups.

Step 2   Think of a real-world situation.

Ellie has 35 photos that she is placing in a photo album.
She will put 5 photos on each page.

Solution   **The sentence 35 ÷ 5 = 7 can describe the number of photo pages needed to hold 35 photos, if there are 5 photos on each page.**

2 COACHED EXAMPLE

Which problem could be solved by using division?

A. There are 27 students and 3 teachers on a field trip. How many people are on the field trip in all?

B. There are 3 tennis balls in each of 9 cans. How many balls are there in all?

C. There are 27 model cars in 3 equal rows. How many cars are in each row?

A quotient is the answer to a _____ problem.

To solve problem A, I need to put _____-size groups of objects together.

So, this is a(n) _____ problem.

To solve problem B, I need to put _____-size groups of objects together.

So, this is a(n) _____ problem.

To solve problem C, I need to _____ objects into _____-size groups. So, this is a(n) _____ problem.

I could solve problem _____ by finding the quotient.

1 Decide if you can use division to solve each problem. Select Yes or No.

A. There are 21 students in a class. They are sitting at tables of 3 for a science experiment. How many tables of students are there?　　○ Yes　○ No

B. Bethany has 12 rocks in her collection. She put the rocks in 2 boxes. One box has 3 rocks. How many rocks are in the other box?　　○ Yes　○ No

C. A string is cut into 6 pieces. Each piece is 2 feet long. How long was the string before it was cut?　　○ Yes　○ No

D. The area model is made from 20 square tiles. There are 5 square tiles in each row. How many rows are there?　　○ Yes　○ No

2 Mrs. Cooper drew the area model shown below on the board.

- Cody wrote 36 ÷ 4 = 9 to represent the area model.
- Isabel wrote 36 ÷ 9 = 4 to represent the area model.

Who is correct? Explain your thinking.

3 Which model represents 15 ÷ 5? Mark all that apply.

○ A.

○ B.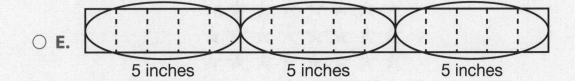

○ C.

○ D.

○ E.

○ F.

4 Draw a line from each problem to the number sentence that represents it.

A. Will has 10 shells. He puts 2 shells • in each box. How many boxes of shells does Will have?

B. Timmy has 10 shells. He gives • 2 shells to a friend. How many shells does Timmy have left?

C. Amy has 10 shells. She puts the • same number of shells in 5 boxes. How many shells are in each box?

D. Zoe has 10 shells in each box. • She has 5 boxes of shells. How many shells does Zoe have?

• $10 - 2 = \square$

• $10 \div 5 = \square$

• $10 \times 5 = \square$

• $10 \div 2 = \square$

5 Read each statement about the array below. Select True or False.

A. The quotient of 48 and 6 tells how many stars are in each row. ○ True ○ False

B. The product of 6 and 8 tells how many stars are in each row. ○ True ○ False

C. You can divide 48 by 8 to find how many rows are in the array. ○ True ○ False

D. The quotient of 8 and 6 tells how many rows are in the array. ○ True ○ False

6 Mark used 16 square tiles to make an area model. He made 4 equal rows. Write a number sentence to show how many tiles are in each row.

_____ ◯ _____ = _____

7 The table shows the sections of fence that a store sells. The sections are different colors and different lengths.

Fence Sections

Color	Length (in feet)
White	6
Tan	5
Brown	3

Mr. Quan wants to build a tan fence that is 30 feet long. How many sections of fence should Mr. Quan buy? Write the number sentence to show your answer.

_____ ◯ _____ = _____

8 Look at the number sentence.

$24 \div 4 = 6$

Use the division sentence to describe a situation.

3.OA.3

Solving Multiplication Problems

1 GETTING THE IDEA

Multiplication can be used to solve real-world problems. You can represent a multiplication problem in many ways. One of the ways is to make a drawing. Drawings you can use to represent multiplication include equal groups, arrays, and area models.

You can also write an **equation**. An equation is a number sentence with an equal sign (=).

Example 1

Mr. Thomas planted 3 rows of pine trees. There are 6 pine trees in each row. How many pine trees did Mr. Thomas plant in all?

Strategy   Make a drawing, then write an equation.

Step 1   Make a drawing.

There are 3 rows of pine trees with 6 trees in each row.

Step 2   Write an equation.

number of rows		number of trees in each row		number of trees in all
3	×	6	=	18

Solution   Mr. Thomas planted 18 pine trees in all.

Example 2

Lisa has a group of square tiles. She has 2 rows of tiles. Each row has 4 tiles. How many total tiles does Lisa have?

Strategy   Make a model, and write an equation.

Step 1   Draw and label a model.

Draw a rectangle to represent the tiles.

Divide the rectangle into 2 equal rows of 4 squares.

The long side has 4 tiles. The short side has 2 tiles.

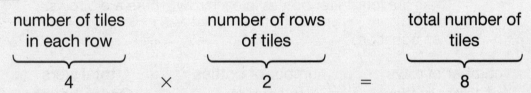

Step 2   Write an equation.

number of tiles in each row		number of rows of tiles		total number of tiles
4	×	2	=	8

Solution   Lisa has 8 total tiles.

You can also use multiplication to solve measurement problems.

Lee used 4 cups of oatmeal to make 1 batch of muffins. How much oatmeal should he use to make 2 batches of muffins?

4 cups × 2 batches = 8 cups

Bev can run 1 mile in 10 minutes. How long would it take her to run 3 miles?

10 minutes × 3 miles = 30 minutes

Example 3

Carlos bought a case filled with 1-liter bottles of water. The case had 5 rows of bottles. There were 4 bottles in each row. How many liters of water did Carlos buy?

Strategy   Make a drawing, and write an equation.

Step 1   Make a drawing.

You can draw an array.

There are four 1-liter bottles in each row. There are 5 rows.

Step 2   Write an equation.

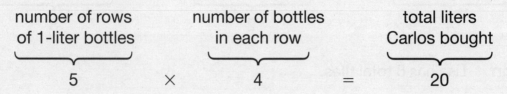

number of rows of 1-liter bottles		number of bottles in each row		total liters Carlos bought
5	×	4	=	20

Solution   Carlos bought 20 liters of water.

Alicia bought 3 boxes of pencils. There were 10 pencils in each box. How many pencils did Alicia buy?

Make a drawing to represent the problem.

There are _____ boxes of pencils. Each box had _____ pencils.

Write an equation.

_____ × _____ = _____

Alicia bought _____ pencils.

1 Ms. Garcia used squares of felt to cover a bulletin board.

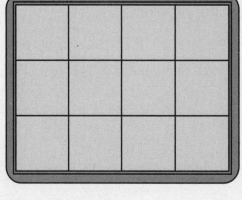

Select True or False for each statement.

A. Each side of the bulletin board has 3 squares of felt.   ○ True   ○ False

B. Multiply 3 × 4 to find the total number of squares of felt.   ○ True   ○ False

C. Ms. Garcia used 7 squares of felt in one row.   ○ True   ○ False

D. Ms. Garcia used 12 total squares of felt in all.   ○ True   ○ False

2 Jenna put 7 marbles into each of 8 bags. How many total marbles does Jenna have? Draw a picture to help you solve the problem.

Equation: _____

Jenna has _____ marbles in all.

3 Students lined up in rows for a photo. Circle numbers to make an equation that shows the total number of students.

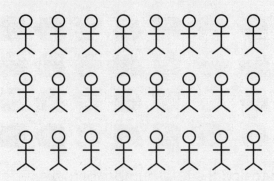

3		6		21	
4	×	7	=	24	students
5		8		28	

4 Sadie made two designs with string. She used 6 pieces in Design A and 8 pieces in Design B. Each piece of string is 9 centimeters long.

How many centimeters of string did Sadie use in each design? Use numbers from the box to complete each equation.

Design A: _____ × 9 centimeters = _____ centimeters

Design B: _____ × 9 centimeters = _____ centimeters

6
8
9
48
54
72

5 Andre arranged his rocks in rows as shown below. Which statement is true? Mark all that apply.

○ **A.** Add 9 and 4 to find the total number of rocks.

○ **B.** Multiply 4 and 9 to find the total number of rocks.

○ **C.** Andre could put that same number of rocks in 6 rows with 6 rocks in each row.

○ **D.** Andre could put that same number of rocks in 5 rows with 8 rocks in each row.

○ **E.** Andre has 32 total rocks.

○ **F.** Andre has 36 total rocks.

6 Emma bought 7 books of stickers. There are 5 pages in each book. How many pages of stickers are in the books in all? Draw a picture to help you solve the problem.

_____ pages

7 Kaleb glued tiles onto trays. Each tile is the same size. The tiles are arranged in the shape of a rectangle.

Tray	Rows	Number of Tiles in Each Row
A	8	8
B	9	7

Which tray has more tiles? Tray _____

How did you compare the trays?

8 Mr. Harper made a gate. He used 4 equal-sized metal bars.

8 feet

What was the total length of metal bars he used?

_____ × _____ = _____ feet

9 There are 10 oranges in a box. How many oranges are in 9 boxes?

Write an equation. _____

_____ oranges

10 Jules trained for soccer and swimming events.

- soccer: 7 weeks for 6 hours each week

- swimming: 9 weeks for 5 hours each week

Select True or False for each statement.

A. Jules trained more hours for swimming than for soccer. ○ True ○ False

B. Jules trained 42 total hours for soccer. ○ True ○ False

C. Jules trained 40 total hours for swimming. ○ True ○ False

D. Jules trained 87 total hours for both sports. ○ True ○ False

Solving Division Problems

1 GETTING THE IDEA

You can solve real-world problems with division. As with multiplication, you can draw a model to show the problem. You can also write an **equation** to solve the problem.

In a division equation, the **dividend** is the number being divided, and the **divisor** is the number you are dividing by. The **quotient** is the solution.

Example 1

Maggie had 18 stamps. She placed an equal number of stamps on 9 letters. How many stamps did Maggie put on each letter?

Strategy   Draw a model, and write an equation.

Step 1   Draw a model of equal groups.

Draw 18 squares to represent stamps.

Make 9 equal groups to represent letters.

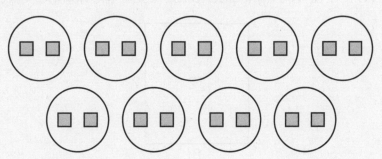

Step 2   Write an equation.

total number of stamps		number of letters		number of stamps on each letter
18	÷	9	=	2

Solution   Maggie put 2 stamps on each letter.

Division can help you solve real-world measurement problems.

Tia wants to practice her violin for 10 hours total over the next 5 days. How many hours should she practice each day?

Tia can divide 10 hours by 5 days.

$$10 \div 5 = 2$$

Tia should practice her violin for 2 hours each day.

Example 2

Ernesto made a digital photo album. The album has 72 photos on each page. All 72 photos are lined up in rows. There are 8 photos in each row. How many rows of photos are there on each page in Ernesto's digital album?

Strategy   Draw a model, and write an equation.

Step 1   Label an area model.

Draw a rectangle to represent each page.

Write 72 inside to represent the total number of photos.

Write 8 on the bottom of the rectangle to represent the number of photos in each row.

Write ? on the right side to represent the number of rows.

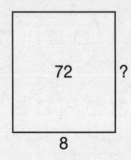

Step 2   Write an equation.

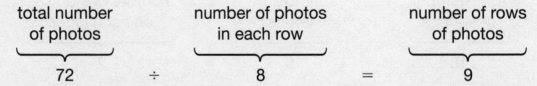

Solution   There are 9 rows of photos on each page.

Example 3

A farmer has 30 pounds of carrots. He put the same number of pounds of carrots in each of 3 boxes. How many pounds of carrots are in each box?

Strategy   Draw a model, and write an equation.

Step 1   Draw an array.

Draw 30 circles to represent 30 pounds.

Make 3 equal rows to represent 3 boxes.

There are 10 circles in each row.

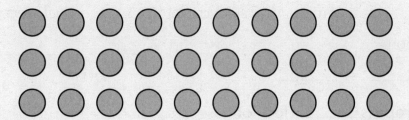

Step 2   Write an equation.

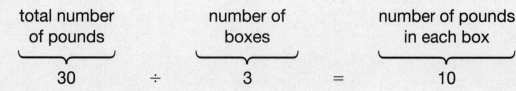

total number of pounds		number of boxes		number of pounds in each box
30	÷	3	=	10

Solution   There are 10 pounds of carrots in each box.

Mr. Taylor cut 35 feet of rope into 5 equal pieces. How long is each piece of rope?

Draw a model to represent the problem.

There are _____ feet of rope. Mr. Taylor cut into _____ equal pieces.

Write an equation.

_____ ÷ _____ = _____

Each piece of rope is _____ feet long.

1 Jessie put cat and dog treats into sacks.

- He divided 42 cat treats equally into 7 sacks.

- He divided 45 dog treats equally into 9 sacks.

How many cat or dog treats are in each sack? Select True or False for each statement.

A. Divide the number of treats for each animal by the number of sacks for each animal to solve.   ○ True   ○ False

B. There are more dog treats in each sack than cat treats.   ○ True   ○ False

C. There are 6 cat treats in each sack.   ○ True   ○ False

D. There are 6 dog treats in each sack.   ○ True   ○ False

2 Mr. Gates paid $56 for 8 tickets to a talent show. How much did each ticket cost?

Equation: _____

Each ticket cost $_____.

3 Mr. Yates built a fence 28 feet long. He built it in 4 sections that are all the same length. How long is each section?

_____ feet

Explain how you solved the problem.

4 Sara put some paint brushes into cups. Select Yes or No to tell whether she can put an equal number of brushes in each cup.

A. 27 brushes in 3 cups   ○ Yes   ○ No

B. 32 brushes in 4 cups   ○ Yes   ○ No

C. 44 brushes in 6 cups   ○ Yes   ○ No

D. 54 brushes in 7 cups   ○ Yes   ○ No

5 Zane had 20 balloons. He tied an equal number of balloons to 5 chairs. How many balloons did Zane tie to each chair?

Make 5 equal groups to represent the problem.

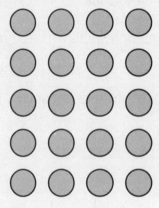

Zane tied _____ balloons to each chair.

6 Rafa has 15 feet of fencing. The fencing is divided into sections that are 3 feet long. How many sections of fencing does Rafa have? Circle the number that makes the statement true.

Rafa has
| 3 |
| 4 |
| 5 |
| 6 |
sections of fencing.

7 Marco and his friends are on vacation. He bought two different types of postcards for his friends to send out. How many postcards did he buy for each friend?

Type of Postcard	Number of Postcards	Number of Friends
Animal	24	8
Park	24	6

Use the numbers in the box to write equations.
Then complete the statements.

Animal postcards: _____ ÷ _____ = _____

He bought _____ animal postcards for each friend.

Park postcards: _____ ÷ _____ = _____

He bought _____ park postcards for each friend.

> 3
> 4
> 5
> 6
> 8
> 12
> 24

8 Pia saw a sign at a yarn store.

> **Yarn Rolls**
>
> 54 yards in 6 rolls
>
> 63 yards in 7 rolls

Pia said you get more yarn for each roll if you buy 7 rolls than if you buy 6 rolls. Is she correct? Explain.

9 Jay placed 40 chairs in the rows shown below.

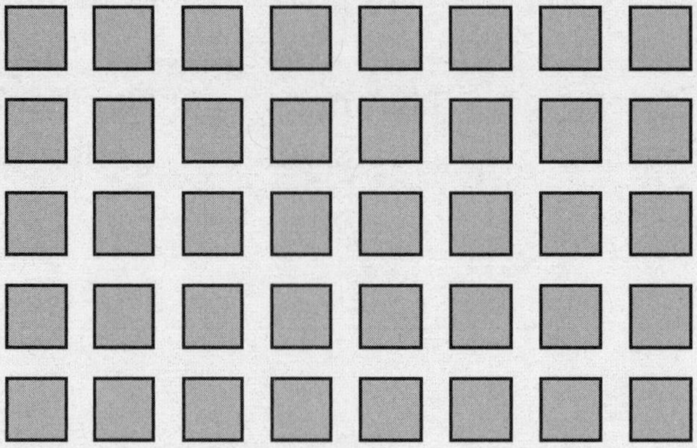

Which statement is true? Mark all that apply.

- **A.** The equation $40 \div 10 = 4$ represents the number of chairs in each row.
- **B.** The equation $40 \div 8 = 5$ represents the number of chairs in each row.
- **C.** Jay could have made 4 rows with 10 chairs in each row.
- **D.** Jay could have made 8 rows with 5 chairs in each row.

10 Abby has 6 pictures of her friends. She placed 2 pictures in each row on her bulletin board. How many rows of pictures of Abby's friends are on her bulletin board? Write an equation to solve.

Equation: _____

Abby has _____ rows of pictures with two pictures in each row on her bulletin board.

Finding Unknown Values

① GETTING THE IDEA

To solve a multiplication equation, you sometimes need to find an unknown number.

The multiplication array below shows 3 rows of 5 dots.

You can use ? to stand for any unknown number in an equation. You can also use a shape, such as a ☐. In a multiplication equation, you may be trying to find an unknown factor or an unknown product.

Unknown Numbers in Multiplication
3 × ? = 15 ⟵ unknown **factor**
? × 5 = 15 ⟵ unknown **factor**
3 × 5 = ? ⟵ unknown **product**

Sometimes, you need to find an unknown number in a division equation.

The division array below shows 15 dots in equal rows of 5.

In a division equation, you can be trying to find an unknown divisor, dividend, or quotient.

Unknown Numbers in Division
15 ÷ ? = 5 ⟵ unknown **divisor**
? ÷ 5 = 3 ⟵ unknown **dividend**
15 ÷ 5 = ? ⟵ unknown **quotient**

Example 1

Mia put 8 stickers in each row. She used 32 stickers on the page.
How many rows of stickers are on the page?

$$8 \times \, ? = 32$$

Strategy   Use an array to find an unknown factor.

Step 1   Draw 8 dots in one row.

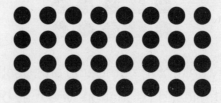

Step 2   Add more rows of 8 dots until you have 32 dots in all.

Step 3   Count how many rows of 8 make 32.

There are 4 rows of 8 dots.

$$8 \times \, ? = 32$$

$$? = 4$$

Solution   There are 4 rows of stickers on the page.

An array that shows a multiplication problem also shows a division problem.
This is because division is the opposite of multiplication.

Look at the array above. It shows that $8 \times 4 = 32$. It also shows that $32 \div 8 = 4$.

Remember, if you know a multiplication fact, you can use it to find a division fact.

$$8 \times \square = 32 \qquad\qquad\qquad 32 \div 8 = \square$$

8 times what number equals 32?   *Into how many rows of 8 can 32 be divided?*

In both equations, $\square = 4$.

Example 2

Kyo has 20 superhero figures. He put an equal number of figures on 4 shelves. How many figures are on each shelf?

$$20 \div \square = 4$$

Strategy   Make a model, and use a multiplication fact.

> **Step 1**   Draw 4 large circles, one for each shelf.

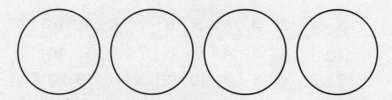

> **Step 2**   Use 20 counters, one for each figure. Place 1 counter in each circle.

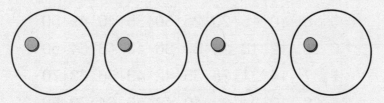

> **Step 3**   Continue placing 1 counter at a time in each circle until you run out of counters.

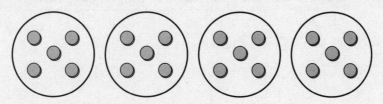

> There are 5 counters in each circle.

> **Step 4**   Use a multiplication fact.
>
> You're looking for $\square$ in $20 \div \square = 4$.
>
> Think about multiplication.
>
> 4 times what number equals 20?
>
> $4 \times 5 = 20$. So $20 \div 4 = 5$.
>
> So, $\square = 5$.

Solution   Kyo puts 5 figures on each shelf.

Since multiplication is the opposite of division, they are called **inverse operations**. This means they are operations that can be used to undo one another.

Example 3

Find the value of $\triangle$.

$$\triangle \div 9 = 6$$

Strategy   Use a multiplication table to find the unknown dividend.

×	1	2	3	4	5	6	7	8	9	10
1	1	2	3	4	5	6	7	8	9	10
2	2	4	6	8	10	12	14	16	18	20
3	3	6	9	12	15	18	21	24	27	30
4	4	8	12	16	20	24	28	32	36	40
5	5	10	15	20	25	30	35	40	45	50
6	6	12	18	24	30	36	42	48	54	60
7	7	14	21	28	35	42	49	56	63	70
8	8	16	24	32	40	48	56	64	72	80
9	9	18	27	36	45	54	63	72	81	90
10	10	20	30	40	50	60	70	80	90	100

Step 1   Identify the parts of the equation.

$$\triangle \quad \div \quad 9 \quad = \quad 6$$

unknown   divisor   quotient
dividend

Step 2   Use multiplication, which is the inverse operation of division.

The dividend is unknown.

You can use the product of a multiplication fact to find the dividend.

You can use $9 \times 6 = \triangle$ to find $\triangle \div 9 = 6$.

Step 3 ▸ Find the product of 9 and 6 in the multiplication table.

Shade the row for 9.
Shade the column for 6.

×	1	2	3	4	5	6	7	8	9	10
1	1	2	3	4	5	6	7	8	9	10
2	2	4	6	8	10	12	14	16	18	20
3	3	6	9	12	15	18	21	24	27	30
4	4	8	12	16	20	24	28	32	36	40
5	5	10	15	20	25	30	35	40	45	50
6	6	12	18	24	30	36	42	48	54	60
7	7	14	21	28	35	42	49	56	63	70
8	8	16	24	32	40	48	56	64	72	80
9	9	18	27	36	45	54	63	72	81	90
10	10	20	30	40	50	60	70	80	90	100

Step 4 ▸ Find the product.

The product is in the square where the shading overlaps.

$9 \times 6 = \triangle$

$\triangle = 54$

Step 5 ▸ Use the product to find the unknown dividend.

The product in the multiplication fact is the same as the dividend in the division equation.

$9 \times 6 = 54$

$\triangle \div 9 = 6$

$\triangle = 54$

Solution $\triangle = 54$

Brianna needs $42. She wants to save $6 each week. How many weeks will she have to save?

$$? \times 6 = 42$$

In this equation, you need to find the unknown _____.

Draw an array. Start by making 1 row of _____ dots.

Keep drawing rows of _____ dots until there are _____ dots in all.

There are _____ rows, with _____ dots in each row.

$? =$ _____

It will take _____ weeks for Brianna to save $42.

1 Use the array below to complete the statement and the equations.

There are _____ rows, with _____ notes in each row.

_____ ÷ _____ = _____ or _____ ÷ _____ = _____

2 Draw a line from each multiplication equation to the division equation with the same answer.

A. $3 \times ? = 21$ •

B. $? \times 8 = 16$ •

C. $6 \times 7 = ?$ •

D. $7 \times ? = 14$ •

• $16 \div 8 = ?$

• $14 \div ? = 7$

• $21 \div ? = 3$

• $? \div 6 = 7$

3 Which equation could this array represent? Mark all that apply.

○ **A.** $4 \times \triangle = 28$ ○ **D.** $4 \times \triangle = 24$

○ **B.** $\triangle \times 4 = 7$ ○ **E.** $\triangle \times 7 = 28$

○ **C.** $7 \times \triangle = 28$ ○ **F.** $\triangle \times 3 = 21$

4 Circle the number for the unknown factor and quotient that make the equations true.

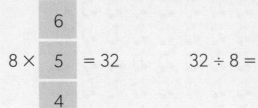

$$8 \times \boxed{\begin{array}{c} 6 \\ 5 \\ 4 \end{array}} = 32 \qquad 32 \div 8 = \boxed{\begin{array}{c} 4 \\ 5 \\ 6 \end{array}}$$

5 Does the value of $\square$ = 6? Select Yes or No.

A. $24 \div \square = 6$ ○ Yes ○ No

B. $30 \div \square = 5$ ○ Yes ○ No

C. $40 \div \square = 8$ ○ Yes ○ No

D. $36 \div \square = 6$ ○ Yes ○ No

E. $63 \div \square = 7$ ○ Yes ○ No

6 Manny solved each equation below. The answer he found is given.
Is Manny's answer correct? Select Yes or No.

A. $\triangle \div 1 = 1$ ○ Yes ○ No
$\triangle = 4$

B. $\square \div 8 = 7$ ○ Yes ○ No
$\square = 56$

C. $? \div 2 = 6$ ○ Yes ○ No
$? = 12$

D. $\triangle \div 5 = 7$ ○ Yes ○ No
$\triangle = 35$

E. $? \div 6 = 8$ ○ Yes ○ No
$? = 49$

7 There are 32 students in Ms. Naples's class. There are 4 students seated at each table. Write the number from the box that makes the statement true.

5
6
7
8
24
32

There are _____ tables for students in Ms. Naples's class.

8 Each equation in the table has an unknown value. Indicate with an "X" whether the equation has an unknown factor, unknown divisor, or unknown dividend.

Equation	Unknown Factor	Unknown Divisor	Unknown Dividend
$\triangle \div 7 = 8$			
$\triangle \times 2 = 8$			
$5 \times \triangle = 25$			
$72 \div \triangle = 9$			
$\triangle \div 4 = 3$			

9 Alex bought some snack packs for lunch.
He bought 2 berry snack packs.
He bought 3 banana snack packs.

Snack Packs	Price per Pack
Banana	$4
Berry	$3

Part A

How much did Alex spend on berry snack packs?

_____ × _____ = ?

? = _____

Alex spent _____ on berry snack packs.

Part B

How much did Alex spend on banana snack packs?

_____ × _____ = ?

? = _____

Alex spent _____ on banana snack packs.

Part C

Alex said that the money he spent on banana snack packs is 2 times more than the money he spent on berry snack packs. Is he correct? Explain your answer.

Multiplication Properties

 GETTING THE IDEA

You can use the properties of multiplication to help you find products.

The **commutative property of multiplication** states that you can change the order of the factors in a multiplication equation without changing the product.

If you don't remember 4×6, try 6×4.

$6 \times 4 = 24$ $4 \times 6 = 24$

The **associative property of multiplication** states that you can change the way you group factors in a multiplication equation without changing the product.

$3 \times 2 \times 4 = ?$

You can multiply 3×2 first, then multiply by 4.

$(3 \times 2) \times 4 = 6 \times 4 = 24$

Or, you can multiply 2×4 first, then multiply by 3.

$3 \times (2 \times 4) = 3 \times 8 = 24$

The **distributive property of multiplication** states that you can break apart a factor in a multiplication equation without changing the product.

If you don't remember 6×7, you can break apart 7 into $5 + 2$.

$6 \times 7 = 6 \times (5 + 2)$

$= (6 \times 5) + (6 \times 2)$

$= 30 + 12$

$= 42$

Example 1

Nadia wants to arrange a group of her photos for a display. She wants to arrange the photos in rows, with the same number of photos in each row. She tried 3 rows with 5 photos in each row. Can she arrange that same group of photos in a different way? Explain.

Strategy Use different arrays to model the same number of objects.

Step 1 Draw an array to show the problem.

Draw 3 rows of 5 squares. Each square is one photo. Each row is one page.

3 rows of 5 or $3 \times 5 = 15$

Nadia has 15 photos.

Step 2 Find another way to arrange the photos in rows, with the same number of photos in each row.

5 rows of 3 or $5 \times 3 = 15$

Step 3 Compare the results.

Nadia can put 3 photos in each of 5 rows.

3 rows of 5 = $3 \times 5 = 15$

She can also put 5 photos in each of 3 rows.

5 rows of 3 = $5 \times 3 = 15$

Solution **Nadia can use 5 rows with 3 photos in each row. Changing the order of the factors shows another way to arrange the photos.**

Example 2

Max needs to multiply $3 \times 2 \times 5$. In what two ways can he find the product?

Strategy   Use arrays to model grouping factors in different ways.

Step 1   Group the first two factors.

$$3 \times 2 \times 5 =$$
$$(3 \times 2) \times 5 =$$

Step 2   Multiply by the third factor.

$$(3 \times 2) \times 5 =$$
$$6 \times 5 = 30$$

Step 3   Change the groupings. Multiply again.

$$3 \times (2 \times 5) =$$
$$3 \times 10 = 30$$

Solution $(3 \times 2) \times 5 = 3 \times (2 \times 5)$

You can solve the problem in Example 2 another way.
Use the commutative property first. Then the associative property.
$$3 \times 2 \times 5 = 3 \times 5 \times 2 = (3 \times 5) \times 2 = 15 \times 2 = 30$$

Example 3

Use the distributive property of multiplication to find the product of 7×9.

Strategy   Use a model to break apart one factor.

Step 1   Draw a rectangle to show 7×9. Break apart 9 into $5 + 4$.

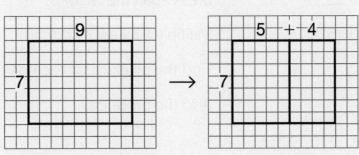

$$7 \times 9 = 7 \times (5 + 4)$$

Step 2   Find the products for each part.

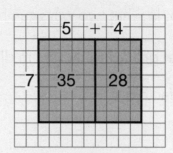

$$7 \times (5 + 4) = (7 \times 5) + (7 \times 4)$$
$$= 35 + 28$$

Step 3   Add the products.

The sum is equal to the total number of squares.

$$35 + 28 = 63$$

Solution $7 \times 9 = 63$

2 COACHED EXAMPLE

Use the distributive property of multiplication to find the product of 5×8.

You can draw a rectangle that shows how to _____ apart a factor.

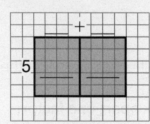

$5 \times 8 = 5 \times (\underline{\quad} + \underline{\quad})$ Break apart the factor 8.

$\quad = (5 \times \underline{\quad}) + (5 \times \underline{\quad})$ Multiply 5 by each addend.

$\quad = \underline{\quad} + \underline{\quad}$ Find the product for each part.

$\quad = \underline{\qquad}$ Add the products.

$5 \times 8 = \underline{\quad}$

1 **Part A**

Look at the model. Write a multiplication equation.

_____ × _____ = _____

Part B

Draw another array that uses the same factors and has the same product. Write an equation for your array.

_____ × _____ = _____

2 Draw a line to connect problems with the same value.

A. 4×9 •

• $4 \times (2 \times 3)$

B. $(4 \times 2) \times 3$ •

• $(4 \times 3) + (2 \times 3)$

C. $(4 + 2) \times 3$ •

• 9×4

D. $3 \times (2 \times 2)$ •

• $(3 \times 2) \times 2$

3 Which problem has a product of 36? Mark all that apply.

○ **A.** $3 \times 4 \times 5$ ○ **D.** 9×4

○ **B.** 4×9 ○ **E.** $4 \times (4 + 2)$

○ **C.** $4 \times 3 \times 3$ ○ **F.** $3 \times (5 + 7)$

4 Does the problem have the same value as 7×8? Select Yes or No.

A. $7 \times (3 + 5)$ ○ Yes   ○ No

B. $7 \times (4 + 4)$ ○ Yes   ○ No

C. $(7 \times 2) + (7 \times 6)$ ○ Yes   ○ No

D. $7 \times (6 + 2)$ ○ Yes   ○ No

E. $(7 \times 3) + (7 \times 3)$ ○ Yes   ○ No

5 Complete the steps to find the product of 7×7. Use the numbers in the box.

$$7 \times 7 = 7 \times (4 + \underline{\hspace{1.5em}})$$
$$= (7 \times \underline{\hspace{1.5em}}) + (7 \times \underline{\hspace{1.5em}})$$
$$= \underline{\hspace{1.5em}} + \underline{\hspace{1.5em}}$$
$$= \underline{\hspace{1.5em}}$$

3
4
7
14
21
28
42
49

6 Is each equation correct? Select True or False.

A. $6 \times 7 = 6 \times (2 + 3)$ ○ True   ○ False

B. $7 \times 5 = 7 \times (2 + 3)$ ○ True   ○ False

C. $7 \times 6 = 7 \times (3 \times 3)$ ○ True   ○ False

D. $4 \times 8 = (4 \times 8) + (4 \times 8)$ ○ True   ○ False

E. $5 \times 7 = (5 \times 2) + (5 \times 5)$ ○ True   ○ False

F. $8 \times 4 = 8 \times (2 + 2)$ ○ True   ○ False

7 Isabella needs to multiply $4 \times 2 \times 5$. What two ways can Isabella use the associative property of multiplication to find the product? Write the equations. Show the product.

One way: _____

Another way: _____

8 Use the numbers in the box to complete each equation.

$2 \times 9 = (2 \times \underline{\quad}) + (2 \times 6)$

$8 \times 5 = \underline{\quad} \times 8$

$5 \times (\underline{\quad} \times 6) = (5 \times 2) \times 6$

$(\underline{\quad} \times 3) \times 2 = 2 \times (3 \times 2)$

$4 \times 7 = 4 \times (5 + \underline{\quad})$

| 2 |
| 3 |
| 4 |
| 5 |

9 Mr. Johnson has colored pencils in jars. He has 8 jars with 7 pencils in each jar.

Part A

How many colored pencils does he have? Write two different equations you could use to solve the problem.

Part B

Use words, numbers, or pictures to explain the two equations.

10 Lauren used 3 teaspoons of sesame seeds to make each bagel. She put the bagels in 2 bags, with 5 bagels in each bag. How many teaspoons of sesame seeds did she use on all the bagels? Write the multiplication equation you can use to solve the problem. Show two ways to find the answer.

Multiplication and Division Facts

1 **GETTING THE IDEA**

There are many strategies you can use to solve multiplication and division facts.

To solve 5×6, you can

- skip count.

  6, 12, 18, 24, 30

  Skip count by 6 five times, so $5 \times 6 = 30$.

- use repeated addition.

  $0 + 6 = 6$ $6 + 6 = 12$ $12 + 6 = 18$ $18 + 6 = 24$ $24 + 6 = 30$

  Add 6 five times, so $5 \times 6 = 30$.

- use doubles.

  $5 \times 6 = (5 \times 3) + (5 \times 3) = 15 + 15 = 30$

  Double 5×3, so $5 \times 6 = 30$.

To solve $30 \div 6$, you can

- use a multiplication fact.

  Since $5 \times 6 = 30$, so $30 \div 6 = 5$.

- skip count backward.

  30, 24, 28, 12, 6

  Skip count backward by 6 five times, so $30 \div 6 = 5$.

- use repeated subtraction.

  $30 - 6 = 24$ $24 - 6 = 18$ $18 - 6 = 12$ $12 - 6 = 6$ $6 - 6 = 0$

  Subtract 6 five times, so $30 \div 6 = 5$.

Example 1

Compare each product to 50. Write the multiplication problem in the correct box.

| 5×9 | 7×7 | 6×8 | 9×6 | 8×7 |

Less Than 50	Greater Than 50

Strategy   Use skip counting or doubles.

Step 1   Use skip counting for 5×9, 7×7, and 8×7.

5×9	9, 18, 27, 36, 45
$5 \times 9 = 45$	$45 < 50$
7×7	7, 14, 21, 28, 35, 42, 49
$7 \times 7 = 49$	$49 < 50$
8×7	Skip count by one more 7: 49, 56
$8 \times 7 = 56$	$56 > 50$

Step 2   Use doubles for 6×8, and 9×6.

6×8	$6 \times 8 = (6 \times 4) + (6 \times 4) = 24 + 24 = 48$
$6 \times 8 = 48$	$48 < 50$
9×6	$9 \times 6 = (9 \times 3) + (9 \times 3) = 27 + 27 = 54$
$9 \times 6 = 54$	$54 > 50$

Solution

Less Than 50	Greater Than 50
$5 \times 9, 7 \times 7, 6 \times 8$	$8 \times 7, 9 \times 6$

Example 2

Draw a line from each division problem to its quotient.

A. $42 \div 7$ •		• 5
B. $81 \div 9$ •		• 6
C. $63 \div 9$ •		• 7
D. $40 \div 8$ •		• 8
E. $64 \div 8$ •		• 9

Strategy   Use skip counting backward or a multiplication fact.

Step 1   Use skip counting for $42 \div 7$ and $40 \div 8$.

$42 \div 7$ 42, 35, 28, 21, 14, 7, 0

Skip counted backward by 7 six times, so $42 \div 7 = 6$.

$40 \div 8$ 40, 32, 24, 16, 8, 0

Skip counted backward by 8 five times, so $40 \div 8 = 5$.

Step 2   Use multiplication facts for $81 \div 9$, $63 \div 9$, and $64 \div 8$.

$81 \div 9$ Since $9 \times 9 = 81$, $81 \div 9 = 9$.

$63 \div 9$ Since $7 \times 9 = 63$, $63 \div 9 = 7$.

$64 \div 8$ Since $8 \times 8 = 64$, $64 \div 8 = 8$.

Solution

A. $42 \div 7$ •		• 5
B. $81 \div 9$ •		• 6
C. $63 \div 9$ •		• 7
D. $40 \div 8$ •		• 8
E. $64 \div 8$ •		• 9

Select a fact you can use to solve the division problem. Mark all that apply.

$56 \div 8$

○ **A.** $8 + 54 = 62$

○ **B.** $8 \times 7 = 56$

○ **C.** $54 - 46 = 8$

○ **D.** $7 \times 7 = 56$

_____ and division are inverse operations.

That means that _____ does the opposite of division.

To divide 56 by _____, think, "_____ times what number equals 56?"

$8 \times$ _____ $= 56$

To solve $56 \div 8$, I can use _____.

1 Draw a line to connect multiplication problems that have the same product.

A. 1 × 10 •   • 6 × 4

B. 4 × 3 •   • 3 × 3

C. 8 × 3 •   • 2 × 5

D. 9 × 1 •   • 2 × 6

2 Circle the numbers that make a true statement.

2 × 9 = 18		18 ÷ 6 = 3
3 × 6 = 18	is	9 × 2 = 81
6 × 2 = 12		9 × 2 = 18

The inverse of **3 × 6 = 18** is **9 × 2 = 81** .

3 Is the product correct? Select Yes or No.

A. 7 × 8 = 56   ○ Yes   ○ No

B. 9 × 6 = 54   ○ Yes   ○ No

C. 8 × 8 = 54   ○ Yes   ○ No

D. 8 × 5 = 45   ○ Yes   ○ No

E. 5 × 7 = 53   ○ Yes   ○ No

F. 9 × 4 = 36   ○ Yes   ○ No

4 Write a multiplication fact you can use to solve the division problem.

81 ÷ 9

_____ × _____ = _____

5 Is the quotient correct? Select True or False.

A. $30 \div 5 = 6$ ○ True   ○ False

B. $20 \div 4 = 5$ ○ True   ○ False

C. $36 \div 9 = 6$ ○ True   ○ False

D. $21 \div 7 = 4$ ○ True   ○ False

E. $24 \div 3 = 8$ ○ True   ○ False

F. $14 \div 2 = 7$ ○ True   ○ False

6 Draw a line from the multiplication or division problem to its product or quotient.

A. $42 \div 6$ •　　　　　• 32

B. 4×8 •　　　　　• 6

C. $36 \div 6$ •　　　　　• 21

D. $35 \div 7$ •　　　　　• 5

E. 3×7 •　　　　　• 7

7 Sofia has 40 pumpkin muffins. She wants to put them in boxes, with an equal amount in each box. Write division facts to show how many muffins she would put in each box.

5 boxes: _____

_____ muffins in each box

8 boxes: _____

_____ muffins in each box

4 boxes: _____

_____ muffins in each box

8 Tom and Tanya each took a quiz.

Part A

Check their work. Circle any wrong answers.

Tanya's Quiz	Tom's Quiz
$6 \times 9 = 54$	$18 \div 2 = 9$
$15 \div 5 = 3$	$5 \times 5 = 25$
$3 \times 6 = 18$	$54 \div 9 = 6$
$32 \div 8 = 6$	$9 \times 6 = 48$
$7 \times 9 = 63$	$27 \div 3 = 9$
$24 \div 8 = 3$	$7 \times 7 = 49$

Part B

Rewrite any incorrect facts with the correct facts. Explain a strategy that can be used to solve each problem.

Tanya:

Tom:

9 Use the numbers in the box to write multiplication problems with products of 8, 16, and 24.

16 as Product	8 as Product	24 as Product

2
3
4
6
8
12

10 Which statement is correct? Select True or False.

A. The product of 2 × 3 is 2 times the product of 3 × 2. ○ True ○ False

B. 7 × 4 has the same product as 4 × 7. ○ True ○ False

C. 9 × 6 has a product that is equal to the dividend in $\triangle \div 9 = 6$. ○ True ○ False

D. The product of 9 × 8 is 2 times the product of 9 × 4. ○ True ○ False

E. 3 × 5 and 5 × 3 are inverse operations. ○ True ○ False

Solving Two-Step Word Problems

1 GETTING THE IDEA

You can solve word problems by writing **equations**. Use a letter to stand for the unknown value. For example:

> There are 12 boys and 13 girls in one class.
>
> How many students are in the class in all?

You need to find how many students in all. Use *s* to represent the total number of students in the equation.

$$12 + 13 = s$$
$$25 = s$$

You can **round** numbers to check that your answer is reasonable. In the problem above, the addends are 12 and 13. Round both addends to 10.

$$12 + 13 =$$
$$10 + 10 = 20$$

Since 20 is close to 25, the answer is reasonable.

Sometimes, a word problem has two steps, and each step may use a different operation. You may need to write two equations to solve this kind of problem.

Example 1

On a nature walk, Tim drew pictures in his notebook of things he saw. He drew 2 leaves on each of 6 pages. He also drew 8 insects. How many total leaves and insects did Tim draw?

Strategy   Write equations.

Step 1   Determine the operations.

You want to find how many total leaves and insects Tim drew.

You can add the number of leaves and the number of insects.

But to find the total number of leaves, you can first multiply.

Step 2   Write an equation to find the number of leaves.

Use l to represent the number of leaves.

The number of leaves on each page	times	the number of pages	equals	the number of leaves.
↓	↓	↓	↓	↓
2	×	6	=	l

Step 3   Solve the equation.

$$2 \times 6 = l$$
$$12 = l$$

Tim drew 12 leaves.

Step 4   Write an equation to find how many total leaves and insects.

Use t to represent the total number of leaves and insects.

The number of leaves	and	the number of insects	equals	the total number of leaves and insects Tim drew.
↓	↓	↓	↓	↓
12	+	8	=	t

Step 5   Solve the equation.

$$12 + 8 = t$$
$$20 = t$$

Tim drew 20 total leaves and insects.

Step 6 Check that your answer is reasonable.

Tim drew 12 leaves and 8 insects.

12 is close to 10. 8 is also close to 10.

$10 + 10 = 20$

The answer is reasonable.

Solution Tim drew 20 total leaves and insects.

Example 2

Rachel picked 42 flowers. She places those flowers in 7 vases, putting the same number of flowers in each vase. Then she gave 4 of those vases of flowers to her friends. How many flowers did Rachel give to her friends?

Strategy Write equations.

Step 1 Determine the operations.

You want to find how many flowers Rachel gave to her friends. You need to multiply the number of vases she gave to her friends times the number of flowers in each vase.

But first, divide to find the number of flowers in each vase.

Step 2 Write an equation to find the number of flowers in each vase.

Use f to represent the number of flowers in each vase.

The number of flowers Rachel picked	divided by	the number of vases	equals	the number of flowers in each vase.
↓	↓	↓	↓	↓
42	÷	7	=	f

Step 3 Solve the equation.

$42 \div 7 = f$

$6 = f$

There are 6 flowers in each vase.

Step 4 Write an equation to find how many flowers Rachel gave to her friends.

Use g to represent the number of flowers Rachel gave to her friends.

The number of vases Rachel gave to her friends	times	the number of flowers in each vase	equals	the number of flowers Rachel gave to her friends.
↓	↓	↓	↓	↓
4	×	6	=	g

Step 5 Solve the equation.

$$4 \times 6 = g$$
$$24 = g$$

Rachel gave 24 flowers to her friends.

Step 6 Check your answer.

Work backward through the problem. Use inverse operations.

Rachel gave 24 flowers to her friends.
Those 24 flowers were in 4 vases.

$24 \div 4 = 6$. There are 6 flowers in each vase

There are 6 flowers in each vase and 7 vases total:
$6 \times 7 = 42$ flowers total.

Rachel picked 42 flowers, so the answer is correct.

Solution Rachel gave 24 flowers to her friends.

② COACHED EXAMPLE

Eli loves model cars. He has 21 red model cars and 14 black model cars. He put the same number of model cars on each of 5 shelves. How many cars did Eli put on each shelf?

Determine the operations.

To find how many total cars Eli put on each shelf, _____ the total number of cars by the number of _____.

But first, _____ to find the total number of _____.

Write and solve an equation to find the _____ number of cars.

Use c to represent the _____.

_____ ◯ _____ = c

_____ = c

Write and solve an equation to find the number of cars _____.

Use m to represent the number of _____.

_____ ◯ _____ = m

_____ = m

Explain how you know that your answer is reasonable.

_____

_____

_____

Eli put _____ cars on each shelf.

1 There are 26 boys and 28 girls in the third grade. They are broken up into teams of six for field day. How many teams are made up of third graders for field day?

Write and solve equations to answer the problem.

There are _____ third-grade teams.

2 Suzi picked 45 apples. She put 5 apples in each bag. Each bag weighs 2 pounds. How many pounds of apples did Suzi pick?

Use numbers and operation signs from the box to complete two different equations that you could use to solve the problem correctly.

Let b = the number of apples in each bag.

_____ ◯ _____ = b

_____ = b

Let p = the total number of pounds.

_____ ◯ _____ = p

_____ = p

| 2 |
| 5 |
| 9 |
| 18 |
| 20 |
| 45 |
| + |
| − |
| × |
| ÷ |

Suzi picked _____ pounds of apples.

3 The school store usually sells T-shirts for $9 each. Today, the shirts are on sale for $2 off. Mr. Morgan buys 4 shirts on sale. How much did Mr. Morgan pay? Select True or False for each statement.

A. Mr. Morgan paid $11 for each shirt. ○ True ○ False

B. To find the sale price of a shirt, subtract $2 from $9. ○ True ○ False

C. To find the amount Mr. Morgan paid, multiply 4 × $9. ○ True ○ False

D. The sale price of a shirt is $8. ○ True ○ False

E. The total that Mr. Morgan paid for his shirts is $28. ○ True ○ False

4 For the first game at a party, the children were separated into 2 teams, with 10 players on each team. For the second game, the same number of children were separated into 4 teams, with the same number of players on each team. How many children are on each team for the second game?

Write and solve equations to answer the problem.

There are _____ children on each team for the second game.

5 Liz makes 8 fruit baskets to give away as gifts. She puts 4 oranges, 3 apples, and 2 bananas in each basket. Select True or False for each statement.

A. There are 9 pieces of fruit in each basket.   ○ True   ○ False

B. There are 17 total pieces of fruit in the baskets.   ○ True   ○ False

C. There are 72 total pieces of fruit in the baskets.   ○ True   ○ False

D. Liz put 48 total pieces of oranges and apples in the baskets.   ○ True   ○ False

E. Liz put 40 total pieces of apples and bananas in the baskets.   ○ True   ○ False

6 A store has 24 jigsaw puzzles to sell. It displays the same number of puzzles on each of 4 shelves. The first customer buys 3 puzzles from the top shelf. How many puzzles are left on the top shelf?

- Jake said there was 1 puzzle left on the shelf.

- Bella said there were 3 puzzles left on the shelf.

Who is correct? _____

What mistake might the person with the wrong answer have made?

7 Lucas visited a national park that had a cave. In the gift shop, Lucas saw these items from the cave that he wanted to buy.

Item	Cost
Arrowhead	$4
Crystal	$2
Flashlight	$9

Lucas bought 7 crystals and a flashlight. How much did Lucas spend?

Part A

Write and solve the first equation needed to answer this problem.

Part B

Write and solve the second equation needed to answer this problem.

Part C

Use words, pictures, or numbers to explain how you know that your answer is reasonable.

Patterns

A **pattern** is an ordered set of numbers, shapes, or objects. There are many different kinds of patterns. Some patterns may increase.

Each number in this pattern is 3 more than the number before it.
The **rule** of the pattern is add 3.

$$+3 \quad +3 \quad +3 \quad +3$$
$$2, \ 5, \ 8, \ 11, \ 14$$

Some patterns may decrease.

Each number in this pattern is 2 less than the number before it.
The rule is subtract 2.

$$-2 \quad -2 \quad -2 \quad -2$$
$$11, \ 9, \ 7, \ 5, \ 3$$

An **odd number** is a whole number that has a 1, 3, 5, 7, or 9 in the ones place.
An **even number** is a whole number that has a 0, 2, 4, 6, or 8 in the ones place.

Notice that the numbers in the decreasing pattern above are all odd.
The numbers in the increasing pattern above alternate between even and odd.

Example 1

What number pattern do the tiles show? Describe the pattern.

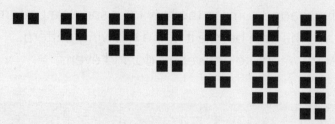

Strategy Count the number of tiles in each set. Find the rule of the pattern.

Step 1 Write the number that each set of tiles represents.

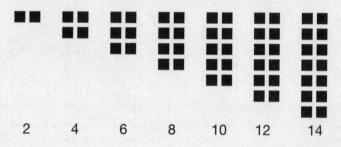

| 2 | 4 | 6 | 8 | 10 | 12 | 14 |

Step 2 Look for a pattern.

Each set of tiles has 2 more tiles than the set before it.
The rule is add 2.

Step 3 Analyze the numbers in the pattern.

The numbers are even numbers.

Solution The tiles show the number pattern 2, 4, 6, 8, 10, 12, 14.
Each number in the pattern is an even number.

In an addition table, the addends are in the first row and column. The sums fill the rest of the table. You can find number patterns in an addition table.

In the table below, the shaded sums in the row for 3 shows a pattern.
Each sum is 1 more than the sum before it. It is a growing pattern.
Also notice that the sums alternate between odd and even.

+	0	1	2	3	4	5	6	7	8	9	10
0	0	1	2	3	4	5	6	7	8	9	10
1	1	2	3	4	5	6	7	8	9	10	11
2	2	3	4	5	6	7	8	9	10	11	12
3	3	4	5	6	7	8	9	10	11	12	13
4	4	5	6	7	8	9	10	11	12	13	14
5	5	6	7	8	9	10	11	12	13	14	15
6	6	7	8	9	10	11	12	13	14	15	16
7	7	8	9	10	11	12	13	14	15	16	17
8	8	9	10	11	12	13	14	15	16	17	18
9	9	10	11	12	13	14	15	16	17	18	19
10	10	11	12	13	14	15	16	17	18	19	20

The shaded sums in the diagonal show another pattern.
Look at each set of addends that make a 10. Other than 5 + 5, there are two sets that use the same addends, just in different orders. This shows the **commutative property of addition**.

$0 + 10 = 10$ $10 + 0 = 10$

$1 + 9 = 10$ $9 + 1 = 10$

$2 + 8 = 10$ $8 + 2 = 10$

$3 + 7 = 10$ $7 + 3 = 10$

$4 + 6 = 10$ $6 + 4 = 10$

$5 + 5 = 10$

Example 2

Look at the shaded sums in the diagonal. What pattern do you see?

+	0	1	2	3	4	5	6	7	8	9	10
0	0	1	2	3	4	5	6	7	8	9	10
1	1	2	3	4	5	6	7	8	9	10	11
2	2	3	4	5	6	7	8	9	10	11	12
3	3	4	5	6	7	8	9	10	11	12	13
4	4	5	6	7	8	9	10	11	12	13	14
5	5	6	7	8	9	10	11	12	13	14	15
6	6	7	8	9	10	11	12	13	14	15	16
7	7	8	9	10	11	12	13	14	15	16	17
8	8	9	10	11	12	13	14	15	16	17	18
9	9	10	11	12	13	14	15	16	17	18	19
10	10	11	12	13	14	15	16	17	18	19	20

Strategy   Analyze the sums and the addends.

Step 1   Write the addends for each sum.

$$0 + 0 = 0 \qquad 3 + 3 = 6 \qquad 6 + 6 = 12 \qquad 9 + 9 = 18$$
$$1 + 1 = 2 \qquad 4 + 4 = 8 \qquad 7 + 7 = 14 \qquad 10 + 10 = 20$$
$$2 + 2 = 4 \qquad 5 + 5 = 10 \qquad 8 + 8 = 16$$

Step 2   Look at each set of addends.

For each sum, the addends are the same.

So these are all doubles facts.

Step 3   Analyze the sums.

Since the facts are doubles, all the sums are even numbers.

Solution   The addends for each sum are the same. The sums are all even numbers.

In a multiplication table, the factors are in the first row and column. The products fill the rest of the table. You can also find many number patterns in a multiplication table.

Example 3

Look at the shaded products in the columns. What pattern do you see?

×	0	1	2	3	4	5	6	7	8	9	10
0	0	0	0	0	0	0	0	0	0	0	0
1	0	1	2	3	4	5	6	7	8	9	10
2	0	2	4	6	8	10	12	14	16	18	20
3	0	3	6	9	12	15	18	21	24	27	30
4	0	4	8	12	16	20	24	28	32	36	40
5	0	5	10	15	20	25	30	35	40	45	50
6	0	6	12	18	24	30	36	42	48	54	60
7	0	7	14	21	28	35	42	49	56	63	70
8	0	8	16	24	32	40	48	56	64	72	80
9	0	9	18	27	36	45	54	63	72	81	90
10	0	10	20	30	40	50	60	70	80	90	100

Strategy   Analyze the products and the factors.

Step 1   Write the facts for some of the products.

$$2 \times 1 = 2 \qquad 6 \times 9 = 54$$
$$8 \times 2 = 16 \qquad 5 \times 8 = 40$$
$$4 \times 2 = 8 \qquad 8 \times 1 = 8$$
$$4 \times 4 = 16 \qquad 10 \times 2 = 20$$
$$7 \times 4 = 28 \qquad 5 \times 10 = 50$$
$$6 \times 3 = 18 \qquad 10 \times 10 = 100$$

Step 2   Look at each set of factors.

Except for 0s, in each set, either one or both factors are even numbers.

Step 3   Analyze the sums.

All of the products are even numbers.

If at least one factor is an even number, the product will be even.

Solution   **When one factor is an even number, the product is an even number.**

Example 4

What pattern was used to make the list below?

17, 14, 11, 8, 5

Strategy   **Find the rule of the pattern.**

Step 1   Do the numbers increase or decrease? Which operation might be used?

The numbers decrease.
Subtraction can be used to make numbers decrease.

Step 2   What number do you subtract from each number to get the next number?

$$17, \quad 14, \quad 11, \quad 8, \quad 5$$
$$-3 \quad -3 \quad -3 \quad -3$$

You subtract 3 to get the next number.
The rule is subtract 3.

Solution   **The rule of subtract 3 was used to make the list of numbers.**

COACHED EXAMPLE

A partial multiplication table is shown below. Look at the shaded products in the rows. What pattern do you see?

×	0	1	2	3	4	5	6	7	8	9	10
0	0	0	0	0	0	0	0	0	0	0	0
1	0	1	2	3	4	5	6	7	8	9	10
2	0	2	4	6	8	10	12	14	16	18	20
3	0	3	6	9	12	15	18	21	24	27	30
4	0	4	8	12	16	20	24	28	32	36	40
5	0	5	10	15	20	25	30	35	40	45	50

List the facts for one row.

_____

_____

Look at each set of factors. What do you notice about each set of factors?

_____

_____

Analyze the products. What do you notice about the products?

_____

_____

When two factors are odd numbers, the product is an _____ number.

When one factor is an odd number, the product may be an _____ number or an _____ number.

1 Find the rule for each pattern. Use a word and number from the box.

A. 10, 8, 6, 4, 2 _____ _____

B. 0, 10, 20, 30, 40 _____ _____

C. 3, 7, 11, 15, 19 _____ _____

D. 16, 13, 10, 7, 4 _____ _____

add
subtract
2
3
4
10

2 Use the addition table below. Select True or False for each statement.

+	0	1	2	3	4	5	6	7	8	9	10
0	0	1	2	3	4	5	6	7	8	9	10
1	1	2	3	4	5	6	7	8	9	10	11
2	2	3	4	5	6	7	8	9	10	11	12
3	3	4	5	6	7	8	9	10	11	12	13
4	4	5	6	7	8	9	10	11	12	13	14
5	5	6	7	8	9	10	11	12	13	14	15
6	6	7	8	9	10	11	12	13	14	15	16
7	7	8	9	10	11	12	13	14	15	16	17
8	8	9	10	11	12	13	14	15	16	17	18

A. The sums in each column show the pattern add 1.　○ True　○ False

B. The sums in each row show the pattern subtract 1.　○ True　○ False

C. A row for an even addend only has even sums.　○ True　○ False

D. A row for an odd addend only has odd sums.　○ True　○ False

3 Which statement describes the pattern? Mark all that apply.

1, 9, 17, 25, 33, 41, 49, 57, 65, 73

○ **A.** All numbers are even.

○ **B.** The rule is subtract 8.

○ **C.** All numbers are odd.

○ **D.** The rule is add 9.

○ **E.** The pattern for the tens digits is 1, 9, 7, 5, 3.

○ **F.** The rule is add 8.

4 Think about multiplication facts. Choose the correct word to make each statement true.

The product of two $\dfrac{\text{even}}{\text{odd}}$ numbers is always an even number.

The product of two odd numbers is always an $\dfrac{\text{even}}{\text{odd}}$ number.

The product of an even number and an odd number is always an $\dfrac{\text{even}}{\text{odd}}$ number.

5 Mrs. Brill wrote the pattern below on the board.

6, 11, 16, 21, 26, 31

- Ramon said that Mrs. Brill used the rule add 5 to make the pattern.

- Erin said that Mrs. Brill used the rule subtract 5 to make the pattern.

Who is correct? _____

What mistake could the other person have made?

```



```

6 This model represents the sum of two odd numbers, 3 + 3.

3   +   3

Part A

Draw models to represent the sum of 3 + 4, 4 + 4, and 4 + 5.

```



```

Part B

Use the drawings to complete each statement.

The sum of two even numbers is always an _____ number.

The sum of two odd numbers is always an _____ number.

The sum of an even number and an odd number is always an _____ number.

```



```

7 Look at the shaded products in the diagonal of the multiplication table below.

×	0	1	2	3	4	5	6	7	8	9	10
0	0	0	0	0	0	0	0	0	0	0	0
1	0	1	2	3	4	5	6	7	8	9	10
2	0	2	4	6	8	10	12	14	16	18	20
3	0	3	6	9	12	15	18	21	24	27	30
4	0	4	8	12	16	20	24	28	32	36	40
5	0	5	10	15	20	25	30	35	40	45	50
6	0	6	12	18	24	30	36	42	48	54	60
7	0	7	14	21	28	35	42	49	56	63	70
8	0	8	16	24	32	40	48	56	64	72	80
9	0	9	18	27	36	45	54	63	72	81	90
10	0	10	20	30	40	50	60	70	80	90	100

Describe the pattern you see in as many ways as possible.

DOMAIN 1 REVIEW

1 Circle a symbol and numbers to make a true sentence about the array.

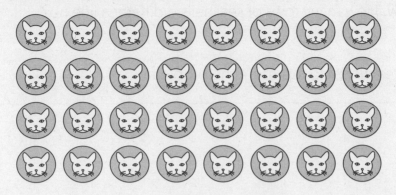

	×	4		16
4	+	8	=	32
	÷	32		36

2 Kara drew the area model below.

Write two division problems the model could represent.
Explain your reasoning.

3 Katrina has 63 seashells. She lined them up in rows. There are 7 seashells in each row. How many rows of seashells did Katrina line up?

Part A

Draw an area model to represent the problem.

Part B

Write an equation to solve the problem.

Equation: _____

Katrina lined up _____ rows of seashells.

4 Is the equation true? Select True or False.

A. $28 \div 7 = 4$ ○ True ○ False

B. $18 \div 3 = 9$ ○ True ○ False

C. $3 \times 4 = 12$ ○ True ○ False

D. $4 \times 9 = 27$ ○ True ○ False

5 Write the numbers to make the equations true.

$6 \times$ _____ $= 48$ $48 \div 6 =$ _____

6 Ione counted 9 turtles at the pond. She counted 3 more frogs than turtles. What is the total number of turtles and frogs Ione counted?

Use numbers and symbols from the box to write two different equations. Then solve the problem.

Let f = the number of frogs. Let n = the total number of turtles and frogs.

_____ ◯ _____ = f

_____ ◯ _____ = n

Ione counted _____ total turtles and frogs.

3	+
9	−
12	×
21	÷
27	

7 Which equation could this array represent? Mark all that apply.

♡ ♡ ♡ ♡ ♡ ♡ ♡
♡ ♡ ♡ ♡ ♡ ♡ ♡
♡ ♡ ♡ ♡ ♡ ♡ ♡
♡ ♡ ♡ ♡ ♡ ♡ ♡
♡ ♡ ♡ ♡ ♡ ♡ ♡
♡ ♡ ♡ ♡ ♡ ♡ ♡

○ **A.** $\triangle \div 6 = 7$

○ **B.** $\triangle \times 7 = 42$

○ **C.** $7 \times \triangle = 49$

○ **D.** $42 \div \triangle = 7$

○ **E.** $\triangle \div 7 = 7$

○ **F.** $6 \times 7 = \triangle$

8 Draw a line from each description to the pattern that describes it. Use the partial multiplication table to help you.

×	0	1	2	3	4	5	6	7	8	9	10
0	0	0	0	0	0	0	0	0	0	0	0
1	0	1	2	3	4	5	6	7	8	9	10
2	0	2	4	6	8	10	12	14	16	18	20
3	0	3	6	9	12	15	18	21	24	27	30
4	0	4	8	12	16	20	24	28	32	36	40
5	0	5	10	15	20	25	30	35	40	45	50

A. the product of an odd factor and the factor 5   •

• repeats even, odd

B. the product of a factor and the factor 3   •

• always even

C. the product of an even factor and another factor   •

• always odd

9 Ryan played soccer 4 days each week for 2 hours each day. He played for 5 weeks in all. How many total hours did Ryan play soccer?

Write the multiplication equation you can use to solve the problem. Then use the associative property of multiplication to show another way to write that same equation.

Ryan played soccer a total of _____ hours.

10 Parker drew this array.

○ ○ ○ ○ ○ ○ ○ ○
○ ○ ○ ○ ○ ○ ○ ○
○ ○ ○ ○ ○ ○ ○ ○

Write a multiplication equation to represent the array.

_____ × _____ = _____

Can Parker use the same numbers to write a multiplication equation
in another way? Explain. Use words and numbers, and name the
property you can use.

11 Tim has 21 action figures. He gave 5 to his little brother. He put the rest on
4 shelves. He put the same number of figures on each shelf. How many action
figures did Tim put on each shelf? Show your work.

There are _____ action figures on each shelf.

12 Write the rule of the pattern below. Then complete the statement about the
numbers in the pattern.

3, 10, 17, 24, 31, ...

Rule: _____

The numbers in the pattern _____.

The County Fair

You have $25 to spend at the county fair. You will use your money to pay for your admission to the fair, ride tickets, and lunch.

Part A For lunch, you may buy up to 3 items. You may buy only 1 of each item.
- List the items you will buy for lunch.
- Write and solve an equation to find how much you will spend for admission and lunch.
- Write and solve an equation to find how much money you will have left for ride tickets.

Part B Use multiplication or division to find the greatest number of sets of ride tickets you can buy with the money you have left after paying for admission and lunch. Will you have any money left over?

Part C Use the number of sets of ride tickets you found in Part B. Write a number pattern to help you find the total number of tickets you can buy. Explain your pattern.

Ride Tickets

Set of 6 $4

Fair Food

Corn on the Cob $2
Corn Dog $4
Chicken Nuggets $3

Drink

Lemonade $2
Bottled Water $1

Part D The table shows how many tickets are needed to go on each ride at the fair.

1 ticket	2 tickets	3 tickets	4 tickets
• carousel	• small Ferris wheel	• swings	• giant Ferris wheel
• giant slide	• teacups	• tilt-a-whirl	• bumper cars

Make a list of the rides you will go on using the rules below. Include how many times you will go on each ride. Explain how you made your list.

- You will go on at least 3 different rides.
- You will go on at least 1 of the 3-ticket rides.
- You will use all of your ride tickets.

Part E Look at your plan for lunch and rides. Will you have money left over after buying tickets and food? What changes, if any, would you make to your plan?

DOMAIN 2

Number and Operations in Base Ten

LESSON 10

Whole Numbers

1 GETTING THE IDEA

You can write whole numbers in different ways.

Standard form: 1,348

Word Form: one thousand, three hundred forty-eight

Expanded Form: 1,000 + 300 + 40 + 8

Place value can help you determine how to write numbers correctly. Place value is the value of a digit based on its position in that number. A place-value chart breaks a number down into individual digits to show their value. This is 1,348 in a place-value chart.

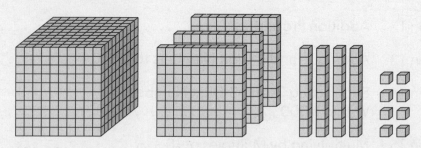

Thousands	Hundreds	Tens	Ones
1,	3	4	8

Example 1

What is the value of each digit in 3,256?

Strategy   Use place-value models and a place-value chart.

Step 1   Model 3,256.

Show thousands, hundreds, tens, and ones.

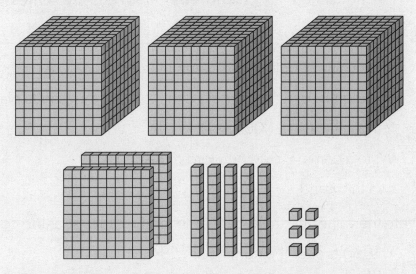

There are 3 thousands, 2 hundreds, 5 tens, and 6 ones.

Step 2   Write 3,256 in a place-value chart.

Use the place-value models in Step 1 to help.

Write a comma after the number in the thousands place.

Thousands	Hundreds	Tens	Ones
3,	2	5	6

Step 3   Find the value of each digit.

The digit 3 has a value of 3,000.
The digit 2 has the value of 200.

The digit 5 has a value of 50.
The digit 6 has a value of 6.

Solution   **The value of each digit is shown in Step 3.**

Example 2

Pia took a plane trip. It was 2,594 miles. Write 2,594 in word form.

Strategy   Use a place-value chart.

Step 1   Write 2,594 in a place-value chart.

Thousands	Hundreds	Tens	Ones
2,	5	9	4

Step 2   Write the value and the word name of the digit before the comma.

The digit before the comma is the 2 in the thousands place.

2 thousands = 2,000

Write a comma after the word *thousand*.

two thousand,

Step 3   Write the value and the word name for the digits after the comma.

The digits after the comma are 594.

5 hundreds = 500   9 tens = 90   4 ones = 4

five hundred ninety-four

Step 4   Write the word name for the whole number.

two thousand, five hundred ninety-four

Solution   The word form of 2,594 is **two thousand, five hundred ninety-four.**

Example 3

A stadium holds 47,903 people. What is 47,903 in expanded form?

Strategy   Use a place-value chart to find the value of each digit.

Step 1   Write 47,903 in a place-value chart.

Write each digit in the chart.
Write a comma after the thousands place.

Ten Thousands	Thousands	Hundreds	Tens	Ones
4	7,	9	0	3

Step 2	Write the value of each digit.

$$40,000 \qquad 7,000 \qquad 900 \qquad 3$$

Step 3	Write the number in expanded form.

Write a + sign between the values of each digit.

Since the tens digit has a 0, you do not have to list the value.

$$40,000 + 7,000 + 900 + 3$$

Solution   The expanded form of 47,903 is $40,000 + 7,000 + 900 + 3$.

② COACHED EXAMPLE

A park had 85,012 visitors. Write 85,012 in word form.

Write the number in a place-value chart.

Ten Thousands	Thousands	Hundreds	Tens	Ones

Write the word name for the value of the digits before the comma.

Write a comma after the word *thousand*.

_____

Next, write the word name for the value of the digits after the comma.

_____

Write the word name for the whole number.

_____

The word form of 85,012 is _____.

1 A movie theater sold 31,809 tickets. Read each statement about the number of tickets. Select True or False.

A. The word form is thirty-one thousand, eighty-nine.　　○ True　○ False

B. The value of the digit 3 is 30,000.　　○ True　○ False

C. The expanded form is 30,000 + 1,000 + 800 + 9.　　○ True　○ False

D. The value of the digit 8 is 80.　　○ True　○ False

E. The tens place has a value of 0.　　○ True　○ False

F. The value of the digit 9 is 90.　　○ True　○ False

2 Draw a line from each place-value model to the number it represents.

A. 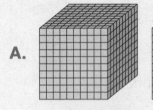 • • 1,032

B. 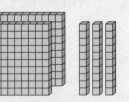 • • 1,230

C. 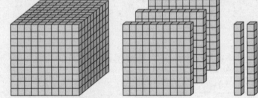 • • 1,302

D. 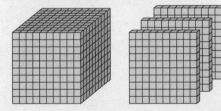 • • 1,320

3 An elephant has a mass of 6,145 kilograms. Write the number of kilograms in word form. Explain how you wrote the number.

4 For each number, write an "X" to show the value of the digit 7.

Number of Letters	70,000	7,000	700	70
57,400				
40,704				
86,973				
73,090				
91,740				

5 A pet shelter received bags of dog food. It received four thousand, eighty-eight bags. Select True or False for each statement.

A. The shelter received 4,088 bags. ○ True ○ False

B. The number of bags can be written as 4,000 + 800 + 8. ○ True ○ False

C. The value of both 8s in the number of bags is the same. ○ True ○ False

D. The expanded form for the number of bags has no hundreds. ○ True ○ False

6 Complete the expanded form for each number.

Standard Form	Expanded Form
40,404	_____ + 400 + _____
40,444	40,000 + _____ + _____ + 4
44,004	40,000 + _____ + _____
44,040	_____ + _____ + 40

7 Felipe and Ava wrote the word form for the number 9,000 + 100 + 1.

Felipe

nine thousand, one hundred one

Ava

nine thousand, one hundred ten

Part A

Who wrote the number in correct word form? _____

Part B

How do you know who wrote the correct word form?

Part C

What error did the other student make?

8 A ballpark has 50,287 seats. Is the word form or expanded form correct? Select Yes or No.

A. fifty thousand, two hundred eighty-seven ○ Yes ○ No

B. 50,000 + 2,000 + 80 + 7 ○ Yes ○ No

C. fifty thousand, twenty-eight hundred seven ○ Yes ○ No

D. 50,000 + 200 + 80 + 7 ○ Yes ○ No

9 Cody used models to represent the length of the Missouri River.

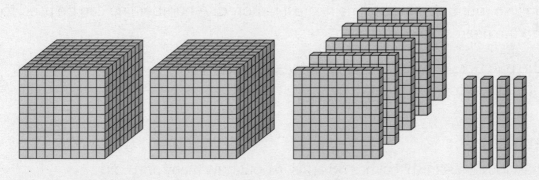

Write the length of the Missouri River in standard form.

_____ miles

10 Mr. Diaz drove his car a certain number of miles. Read the clues to find how many miles he drove.

- There is a 2 in the hundreds place.

- The value of the digit in the ten thousands place is 20,000.

- The digit in the tens place has a value of 60.

- The digit 8 is used twice in the number.
  It has a value of 8,000 and a value of 8.

_____ miles

Rounding Whole Numbers

1 GETTING THE IDEA

When you **round** a number, you are finding a number close to that number.
The rounded number tells *about* how many or *about* how much.

Liz has 12 leaves. She says she has about 10 leaves.
The word *about* means that the number 10 is close to 12.
Liz rounded 12 to the nearest ten.

You can also round numbers to the nearest hundred. A number line can be used to
round to the nearest 10 or 100.

Place the number you want to round between two rounded numbers, and determine
which it is closer to.

Example 1

A scientist found a starfish that has 38 arms. About how many arms did
the starfish have?

Strategy Use a number line.

Step 1 Locate 38 on a number line.

Label the tens. 38 is between 30 and 40.
The first mark is 30. The last mark is 40.

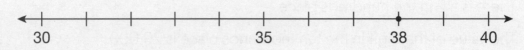

Step 2 Identify the nearest ten.

The middle number is 35. 38 is greater than 35.

38 is closer to 40 than to 30.

The nearest ten is 40.

38 rounded to the nearest ten is 40.

Solution The starfish had about 40 arms.

Rounding rules can also help you round to the nearest ten or hundred.
First, find the place you are rounding to (tens, hundreds). Then look at the digit to the right of that place.

- If that digit is less than 5, do not change the digit in the rounding place.

- If that digit is 5 or greater, increase the digit in the rounding place by 1.

- Change all the digits to the right of the rounding place to 0.

Example 2

Kiri scored 873 points in a season. Round 873 to the nearest ten, and the nearest hundred.

Strategy	Use rounding rules.
Step 1	Find the tens place. Then look at the digit to the right of the tens.

8**7**3

The digit to the right of the tens is 3.

Step 2	Apply the rounding rules.

3 is less than 5, so do not change the digit 7 in the rounding place.

Change the 3 in the ones place to 0.

873 rounded to the nearest ten is 870.

Step 3	Find the hundreds place. Then look at the digit to the right of the hundreds.

87̲3

The digit to the right of the hundreds is 7.

Step 4	Apply the rounding rules.

7 is greater than 5. Increase the digit 9 in the rounding place by 1.

Change the 7 in the tens place and the 3 in the ones place to 0s.

873 rounded to the nearest hundred is 900.

Solution	To the nearest ten, Kiri scored about 870 points. To the nearest hundred, Kiri scored about 900 points.

Example 3

Round the numbers to the nearest hundred. Which numbers round to 600?

554

627

662

Strategy   Use rounding rules.

Step 1   Round 554 to the nearest hundred.

5_5_4

The digit to the right of the rounding place is 5.

5 is equal to 5.

Increase the digit 5 in the rounding place to 6.

Change the digits to the right of the hundreds place to 0.

554 rounds to 600.

Step 2   Round 627 to the nearest hundred.

6_2_7

The digit to the right of the rounding place is 2.

2 is less than 5.

Keep the 6 in the hundreds place the same.

Change the digits to the right of the hundreds place to 0.

627 rounds to 600.

Step 3   Round 662 to the nearest hundred.

6_6_2

The digit to the right of the rounding place is 6.

6 is greater than 5.

Increase the digit 6 in the rounding place to 7.

Change the digits to the right of the hundreds place to 0.

662 rounds to 700.

Solution   **Rounded to the nearest hundred, the numbers 554 and 627 round to 600.**

Tess wanted to round some numbers to the nearest hundred.
Which numbers round to 200?

151

278

245

You are rounding to the nearest _____.

If the digit to the right of the place you are rounding to is less than 5, the digit in the

rounding place _____.

If the digit to the right of the place you are rounding to is 5 or greater, the digit in the

rounding place _____.

Change all digits to the right of the rounding place to _____.

151 rounds to _____ because the digit to the right of the rounding place is _____.

278 rounds to _____ because the digit to the right of the rounding place is _____.

245 rounds to _____ because the digit to the right of the rounding place is _____.

**Rounded to the nearest hundred, the numbers _____
round to 200.**

1 Round 536 to the nearest ten. Then round it to the nearest hundred. Select True or False for each statement.

A. When rounding to the nearest ten, the digit in the tens place stays the same.　　○ True　○ False

B. When rounding to hundreds place, the rounded number is greater than 536.　　○ True　○ False

C. When rounding to the tens place, the rounded number is greater than 536.　　○ True　○ False

D. When rounding to the nearest hundred, the digit in the hundreds place stays the same.　　○ True　○ False

2 On safari, Jacob saw 63 monkeys in a troop. About how many monkeys are in that troop? Use the number line to round 63 to the nearest ten.

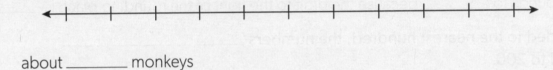

about _____ monkeys

3 Round each number to the nearest hundred and the nearest ten. Write the correct number from the box in the table.

Number	Rounded to Nearest Hundred	Rounded to Nearest Ten
397		
345		
386		
338		

300
340
350
380
390
400

4 Miguel has 68 crayons. About how many crayons does he have? Describe the strategy you used to round.

about _____ crayons

5 Look at each set of numbers. For which set can all of the numbers be rounded to 100? Mark all that apply.

- ○ **A.** 52, 68, 81
- ○ **B.** 49, 74, 93
- ○ **C.** 98, 115, 132
- ○ **D.** 84, 108, 154
- ○ **E.** 126, 137, 133
- ○ **F.** 119, 142, 161

6 Ms. Hoy has a sheep farm. To the nearest hundred, she has about 500 sheep. To the nearest ten, she has about 540 sheep.
How many sheep could Ms. Hoy have? Circle the number that makes the statement true.

Ms. Hoy could have | 505 |
| 535 | sheep.
| 545 |

7 Round each number to the nearest ten. Draw a line from each number to the rounded number.

A. 15 •   • 10

B. 26 •   • 20

C. 14 •   • 30

D. 37 •   • 40

8 Josie counted the stickers in each of her sticker books. She rounded the number to the nearest hundred. Write an "X" to show if the number can be rounded to 100 or 200.

Number of Stickers	Rounded to 100	Rounded to 200
148		
157		
141		
153		

9 Eli has about 290 coins. Could he have the number of coins shown? Select Yes or No.

A. 286   ◯ Yes ◯ No

B. 294   ◯ Yes ◯ No

C. 281   ◯ Yes ◯ No

D. 300   ◯ Yes ◯ No

10 A sea lion weighs 447 pounds. About how much does it weigh?

Round to the nearest hundred and nearest ten. Use the tiles to write the numbers.

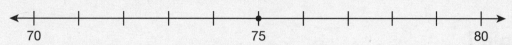

| 0 | 3 | 4 | 5 |

Rounded to nearest hundred: about _____ pounds

Rounded to nearest ten: about _____ pounds

11 Gia has 75 marbles. She used a number line to round 75.

Gia says she can round to 70 or 80 because 75 is in the middle.
Is Gia correct? Explain your answer. Use words and numbers.

Addition Properties

1 GETTING THE IDEA

The numbers that are added in addition are called **addends**. There are several addition properties you can use to help you find sums of addends.

In an addition equation, you can change the order of the addends without changing the sum. This is the **commutative property of addition**.

$$11 + 15 = 15 + 11$$

Example 1

Jai has 13 headbands. She has 11 barrettes. Jai wants to know the total number of headbands and barrettes she has. Show two ways to find the total. Explain your answer.

Strategy   Use the commutative property of addition.

Step 1   Add 13 + 11.

$$13 + 11 = 24$$

Jai has a total of 24 headbands and barrettes.

Step 2   Add 11 + 13.

$$11 + 13 = 24$$

Jai still has a total of 24 headbands and barrettes.

Step 3   Explain why you can use two ways to find the total.

The commutative property of addition says you can change the order of the addends and the sum will be the same.

$$13 + 11 = 11 + 13$$
$$24 = 24$$

Solution   13 + 11 or 11 + 13 can both be used to find Jai's total number of headbands and barrettes.

Another addition property can help you find sums. The **associative property of addition** says that you can group the addends in different ways and the sum will be the same.

$$17 + (13 + 12) = (17 + 13) + 12$$

Group the addends that are easy to add, then find the sum.

Example 2

Tyler wants to add $16 + 14 + 30$. How can he group the addends to find the sum? Determine if there is another way of grouping the addends that is easier to add.

Strategy   Use the associative property of addition.

Step 1   Group the first two numbers.

$$16 + 14 + 30 = (16 + 14) + 30$$

Step 2   Add

$$(16 + 14) + 30 = 30 + 30$$
$$= 60$$

Step 3   Group the second two numbers.

$$16 + 14 + 30 = 16 + (14 + 30)$$

Step 4   Add.

$$16 + (14 + 30) = 16 + 44$$
$$= 60$$

Step 5   Decide which group of addends is easier to add.

You can choose $(16 + 14) + 30$ or $16 + (14 + 30)$. They both have the same sum.

But $(16 + 14) + 30$ is easier to add because you are adding multiples of ten. $30 + 30 = 60$

Solution   **Tyler can add $(16 + 14) + 30$ or $16 + (14 + 30)$ because they both have the same sum, 60. It is easier to add $(16 + 14) + 30$.**

The **distributive property** can help with numbers that are difficult to add. This property says that multiplying a sum by a number is the same as multiplying each addend by the number and then adding the products.

You can rewrite the addends using multiplication facts that share a factor.

$$72 + 24$$
$$\downarrow \qquad \downarrow$$
$$\mathbf{8} \times 9 + \mathbf{8} \times 3$$

Then you can write the problem as a factor shared by both addends times a sum of two addends.

$$\mathbf{8} \times 9 + \mathbf{8} \times 3 = 8 \times (9 + 3)$$
$$72 + 24 = 8 \times (9 + 3)$$
$$72 + 24 = 8 \times (12)$$
$$72 + 24 = 96$$

Example 3

Find the sum of 36 + 27.

Strategy   **Use the distributive property.**

Step 1   Rewrite the addends using multiplication facts that share a factor.

9 is a factor of both 36 and 27.

$$9 \times 4 = 36$$
$$9 \times 3 = 27$$

Step 2   Write the problem as a factor times a sum.

Since 9 is a factor in the multiplication facts for 36 and 27, use 9 as the factor.

The other two factors are 4 and 3. Write 4 + 3 as a sum.

$$9 \times (4 + 3)$$

Step 3   Find the product.

$$9 \times (4 + 3) = 9 \times 7$$
$$= 63$$

Step 4   Write the sum.

$$36 + 27 = 9 \times (4 + 3)$$

$$9 \times (4 + 3) = 63, \text{ so } 36 + 27 = 63.$$

Solution   **$36 + 27 = 63$**

---

❷ COACHED EXAMPLE

Use the distributive property to find the sum of $45 + 27$.

First, rewrite the addends using multiplication facts that share a factor.

_____ is a factor of both 45 and 27.

_____ × _____ = 45

_____ × _____ = 27

Next, write the problem as the shared factor times a sum.

_____ × (_____ + _____)

Last, solve the problem.

_____ × (_____ + _____) = _____ × _____

$$= \underline{\hspace{2em}}$$

The sum of $45 + 27$ is _____.

$45 + 27 = \underline{\hspace{2em}}$

1 Does the equation show the associative property of addition? Select Yes or No.

A. $(28 + 20) + 25 = 28 + (20 + 25)$ ○ Yes ○ No

B. $40 + 32 = 8 \times (5 + 4)$ ○ Yes ○ No

C. $24 + (16 + 52) = (24 + 16) + 52$ ○ Yes ○ No

D. $12 + 14 + 18 = 12 + 18 + 14$ ○ Yes ○ No

2 A circus sold balloons at each show. The colors and the number of balloons sold at Saturday's show are in the table.

Color of Balloon	Number of Balloons Sold
Green	18
Red	25
Yellow	75

Find the total number of balloons the circus sold. Place parentheses around two of the addends that might make the problem easier to solve. Then solve.

$18 + 25 + 75 = $ _____ $+ ($ _____ $+$ _____ $)$

_____ balloons

3 Look at the equation shown below.

$49 + 14 = 7 \times (7 + 2)$

Circle the property that makes the statement true.

associative

The equation shows the   commutative   property.

distributive

4 Juan needs to find $18 + 27$. Select True or False to show whether Juan can use the equation to find the sum.

A. $27 + 18$ ○ True ○ False

B. $18 + (2 + 7)$ ○ True ○ False

C. $3 \times (9 + 2)$ ○ True ○ False

D. $9 \times (2 + 3)$ ○ True ○ False

5 Use numbers from the box to complete each equation.

$(28 + 55) + 45 = 28 + (55 + \underline{\quad})$

$86 + \underline{\quad} = 45 + 86$

$\underline{\quad} + 14 = 7 \times (4 + 2)$

28
35
42
45
55

6 Elena needs to find the sum for the addition problem below.

17 + 26 + 24

Rewrite the equation so that it is easier to find the sum. Use the tiles to write the equation.

| (|) | + | 1 | 2 |

| 3 | 4 | 5 | 6 | 7 |

Equation: _____ = _____

7 Look at each equation in the table. Which property does it show? Write an "X" to show the property.

Equation	Associative Property	Commutative Property	Distributive Property
42 + 18 = 6 × (7 + 3)			
27 + 18 + 32 = 27 + (18 + 32)			
29 + 18 = 18 + 29			

8 Zeke paid a total of $31 for two shirts. One shirt cost $16. The other shirt cost $15. Zeke said he used the distributive property to find the sum. Is this possible? Use words and numbers to explain.

9 In the morning, Kaye rode on two rides at the fair. One ride cost 24 tickets. Another ride cost 18 tickets. She added to find she had used a total of 42 tickets.

Part A

In the afternoon, Kaye rode two more rides. One ride cost 18 tickets. The other ride cost 24 tickets. Kaye said she knew she used 42 tickets without having to add the numbers. Is she correct? How could Kaye know she used a total of 42 tickets?

Part B

Is there another property Kaye could use to find the sum of 42 tickets? Explain your answer.

Adding 2- and 3-Digit Numbers to 1,000

1 GETTING THE IDEA

When you add, the numbers you add are the **addends**. The total is the **sum**.

$8 + 6 = 14$

addends   sum

Often times you will need to **regroup**. That means to replace one amount with another amount of the same value, such as you can regroup 10 ones as 1 ten.

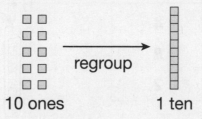

10 ones   regroup   1 ten

Example 1

Li picked 24 apples. Tim picked 18 apples. How many apples did Li and Tim pick in total?

Strategy   Use a place-value chart and place-value models.

Step 1   Write the numbers in a place-value chart. Use place-value models.

	Tens	Ones
	2	4
+	1	8

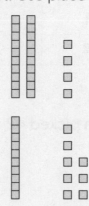

Step 2	Add the ones.

	Tens	Ones
	2	**4**
+	1	**8**

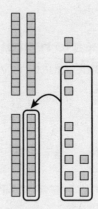

$$4 + 8 = 12$$

Step 3	Regroup the ones.

	Tens	Ones
	1	
	2	**4**
+	1	**8**
		2

12 ones = 1 ten 2 ones

Step 4	Add the tens. Make sure to include the regrouped ten.

	Tens	Ones
	1	
	2	4
+	**1**	8
	4	2

Solution Li and Tim picked 42 apples in all.

Sometimes, you can add numbers mentally.

Example 2

Find the sum.

$35 + 40 + 30$

Strategy   **Group numbers that are easy to add.**

Step 1   Find a pair of numbers you can add mentally.

40 and 30 are easy to add mentally.

4 tens and 3 tens are 7 tens.

$40 + 30 = 70$

$35 + (40 + 30) =$

$35 + 70$

Step 2   Add the third number.

You can count on by tens. Then add the ones

35 is 3 tens and 5 ones.

From 70, count on 3 tens.

$70 \longrightarrow 80, 90, 100$

Then add the ones

$100 + 5 = 105$

Solution $35 + 40 + 30 = 105$

Ten tens are the same as 1 hundred. You can regroup 10 tens as 1 hundred.

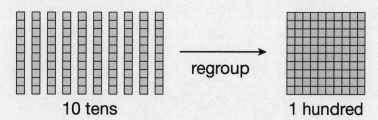

10 tens   regroup   1 hundred

Example 3

Tom walked 148 steps from the bus to his school. He walked 175 steps from his school to the playground. How many total steps did Tom walk?

Strategy   Use a place-value chart.

Step 1   Write the numbers in a place-value chart.

	Hundreds	Tens	Ones
	1	4	8
+	1	7	5

Step 2   Add the ones. Regroup if needed.

$8 + 5 = 13$

13 ones = 1 ten 3 ones

	Hundreds	Tens	Ones
		1	
	1	4	**8**
+	1	7	**5**
			3

Step 3   Add the tens. Regroup if needed.

$1 + 4 + 7 = 12$

12 tens = 1 hundred 2 tens

Hundreds	Tens	Ones
1	1	
1	**4**	8
+ 1	**7**	5
	2	3

Step 4   Add the hundreds.

$1 + 1 + 1 = 3$

Hundreds	Tens	Ones
1	1	
1	4	8
+ **1**	7	5
3	2	3

Solution   Tom walked 323 total steps.

Ana's class raised $357 for a school trip. Ethan's class raised $293. How much money did the two classes raise in all?

To find how much money was raised in all, you need to _____.

Use a place-value chart.

Hundreds	Tens	Ones

+

Add the numbers in the _____ place. Will you need to regroup? _____

Add the numbers in the _____ place. Will you need to regroup? _____

Add the numbers in the _____ place.

The two classes raised $ _____ in all.

1 Draw a line from each number to a number with the same value.

A. 38 ones •   • 3 hundreds 8 tens

B. 83 tens •   • 8 hundreds 3 tens

C. 38 tens •   • 8 tens 3 ones

D. 83 ones •   • 3 tens 8 ones

2 Juan made 17 paper airplanes. Beth made 15 paper airplanes.
The models show how many planes each person made.

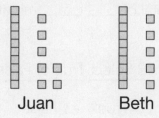

Juan   Beth

Draw a model that shows the total number of airplanes.

Juan and Beth made a total of _____ paper airplanes.

3 Do you need to regroup to add the numbers? Select Yes or No.

A. 34 + 18   ○ Yes   ○ No

B. 671 + 128   ○ Yes   ○ No

C. 452 + 161   ○ Yes   ○ No

D. 73 + 26   ○ Yes   ○ No

4 Lela walked her dog for 28 minutes in the morning. She walked her dog for 34 minutes in the afternoon. How many minutes did Lela walk her dog in all? Use the place-value chart to solve.

Tens	Ones
+	

Lela walked her dog for a total of _____ minutes.

5 Is each number sentence true? Select True or False.

A. $67 + 12 = 89$ ○ True ○ False

B. $45 + 38 = 83$ ○ True ○ False

C. $235 + 225 = 460$ ○ True ○ False

D. $492 + 426 = 818$ ○ True ○ False

6 Sara has a jar of 43 coins. There are 18 quarters and 12 dimes. The rest of the coins are nickels. Circle the number of nickels to make the sentence true.

$$18 + 12 + \boxed{\begin{matrix} 3 \\ 13 \\ 23 \end{matrix}} = 43$$

7 Eli read two books. One book has 298 pages. The other book has 246 pages. He added using the place-value chart below.

Hundreds	Tens	Ones
1	1	
2	9	8
+ 2	4	6
5	5	4

Did Eli add correctly? Explain.

8 Find the missing digits. Use the numbers from the box.

Hundreds	Tens	Ones		
1	1			3
☐	7	5		4
+ 3	☐	8		5
8	4	3		6
				8

9 Drew has already saved $178 to buy a bike. He needs another $137. How much does the bike cost? Show your work.

The bike costs $_____.

10 Use the tiles to write two addends that make up the sum.

| 88 | 97 | 139 | 149 | 168 |

	Hundreds	Tens	Ones
+			
	2	4	6

Subtracting 2- and 3-Digit Numbers Within 1,000

1 GETTING THE IDEA

In a subtraction problem, the number being subtracted from is the **minuend**. The number that you are subtracting is the **subtrahend**. The answer is the **difference**.

$$14 - 8 = 6 \leftarrow \text{difference}$$

minuend   subtrahend

Sometimes, you have to regroup when doing subtraction problems. Since 1 ten is the same as 10 ones, you can regroup 1 ten as 10 ones.

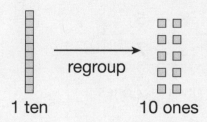

1 ten   regroup   10 ones

Example 1

Sara lives 32 miles from the zoo. Ling lives 15 miles from the zoo. How much farther from the zoo is Sara than Ling?

Strategy   Use a place-value chart and place-value models.

Step 1   Write the numbers in a place-value chart. Use place-value models.

	Tens	Ones
	3	2
−	1	5

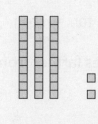

Step 2 Regroup the ones.

You cannot subtract 5 ones from 2 ones.
So, regroup 1 ten as 10 ones.

Tens	Ones
2	12
3̸	2̸
− 1	5

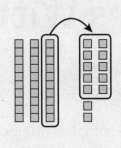

3 tens 2 ones = 2 tens 12 ones

Step 3 Subtract the ones.

Tens	Ones
2	12
3̸	2̸
− 1	5
	7

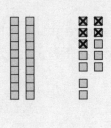

12 ones − 5 ones = 7 ones

Step 4 Subtract the tens.

Tens	Ones
2	12
3̸	2̸
− 1	5
1	7

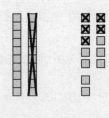

2 tens − 1 ten = 1 ten

Solution Sara is 17 miles farther from the zoo than Ling.

You can also regroup hundreds as tens. One hundred is the same as 10 tens.

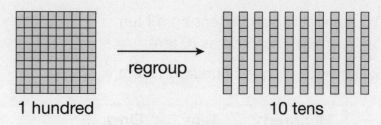

1 hundred   →   10 tens

Example 2

Andy has $215. He spends $62 on a video game. How much money does Andy have left after he buys the video game?

Strategy Use a place-value chart.

Step 1 Write the numbers in a place-value chart.

Hundreds	Tens	Ones
2	1	5
−	6	2

Step 2 Subtract the ones.

5 ones − 2 ones = 3 ones

There are enough ones. You do not need to regroup.

Hundreds	Tens	Ones
2	1	**5**
−	6	**2**
		3

Step 3 ▶ Regroup the tens.

You cannot subtract 6 tens from 1 ten.
So, regroup 1 hundred as 10 tens.

2 hundreds 1 ten = 1 hundred 11 tens

Hundreds	Tens	Ones
1	**11**	
2̸	1̸	5
−	6	2
		3

Step 4 ▶ Subtract the tens.

11 tens − 6 tens = 5 tens

Hundreds	Tens	Ones
1	**11**	
2̸	1̸	5
−	**6**	2
	5	3

Step 5 ▶ Subtract the hundreds.

1 hundred − 0 hundreds = 1 hundred

Hundreds	Tens	Ones
1	11	
2̸	1̸	5
−	6	2
1	5	3

Solution   Andy has $153 left after he buys the video game.

Addition and subtraction are **inverse operations**. They are operations that undo each other. That means you can write a related addition problem for any subtraction problem.

The subtraction problem below starts with the minuend, 8. You subtract the subtrahend, 5, to get a difference of 3.

$$8 - 5 = 3 \leftarrow \text{difference}$$

minuend   subtrahend

To undo the subtraction, start with the difference, 3. Add the subtrahend, 5, to get back to the minuend, 8.

$$3 + 5 = 8$$

You can use this relationship to check your answer to any subtraction problem.

Example 3

At East Park Elementary, there are 325 second graders and 278 third graders. How many more second graders than third graders are there?

Strategy   Use a place-value chart.

Step 1   Write the numbers in a place-value chart.

Hundreds	Tens	Ones
3	2	5
− 2	7	8

Step 2 Subtract the ones. Regroup if needed.

2 tens 5 ones = 1 ten 15 ones

15 ones − 8 ones = 7 ones

Hundreds	Tens	Ones
	1	15
3	2̶	5̶
− 2	7	8
		7

Step 3 Subtract the tens. Regroup if needed.

3 hundreds 1 ten = 2 hundreds 11 tens

11 tens − 7 tens = 4 tens

Hundreds	Tens	Ones
	11	
2	1̶	15
3̶	2̶	5̶
− 2	7	8
	4	7

Subtract the hundreds.

2 hundreds − 2 hundreds = 0 hundreds

Hundreds	Tens	Ones
	11	
2	1̸	15
3̸	2̸	5̸
− 2	7	8
	4	7

Step 5 Use addition to check your answer.

Add the difference to the subtrahend. The sum should be the minuend.

Hundreds	Tens	Ones
1	1	
	4	7
+ 2	7	8
3	2	5

The sum matches the minuend. The answer is correct.

Solution There are 47 more second graders than third graders.

This weekend, Greg watched a movie that was 125 minutes long. Cassie watched a movie that was 142 minutes long. How much longer was the movie that Cassie watched than the movie Greg watched?

To find how much longer Cassie's movie was, I will subtract _____ from _____ .

Write the numbers in the place-value chart. Then find the difference.

	Hundreds	Tens	Ones
−			

First, subtract the _____. Will you need to regroup? _____

Next, subtract the _____. Will you need to regroup? _____

Finally, subtract the _____.

Check your answer using addition.

	Hundreds	Tens	Ones
+			

Cassie's movie was _____ minutes longer than Greg's movie.

1 Use the tiles to name the parts of the subtraction problem.

497 _____

− 154 _____

343 _____

difference	product	subtrahend

addend	sum	minuend

2 Frank did chores for 82 minutes on Saturday and for 45 minutes on Sunday.
How much longer did Frank do chores on Saturday than on Sunday?
Use the place-value chart.

Tens	Ones

Frank did chores for _____ more minutes on Saturday than on Sunday.

3 Do you need to regroup to subtract the numbers? Select Yes or No.

A. 435 − 21   ○ Yes ○ No

B. 928 − 645   ○ Yes ○ No

C. 382 − 181   ○ Yes ○ No

D. 764 − 80   ○ Yes ○ No

4 Raj subtracted 257 from 682 to get the difference 425. What addition problem should you use to check Raj's answer?

_____ + _____ = _____

Is Raj's answer correct? Explain why or why not.

```
┌─────────────────────────────────────────────────────────────┐
│                                                             │
│                                                             │
│                                                             │
│                                                             │
└─────────────────────────────────────────────────────────────┘
```

5 Erin is reading a book with 453 pages. She has read 184 pages so far. How many pages does Erin have left to read? Use the place-value chart.

Hundreds	Tens	Ones

Erin has _____ pages left to read.

6 Find the missing digits or numbers. Use the numbers from the box.

Hundreds	Tens	Ones
	6	☐
☐	7̶	5̶
− 4	☐	9
4	0	☐

15
13
12
8
6
4

7 Draw a line from each subtraction problem to its related addition problem.

A. $73 - 24 = 49$ •

B. $92 - 37 = 55$ •

C. $42 - 29 = 13$ •

D. $74 - 59 = 15$ •

• $55 + 37 = 92$

• $15 + 59 = 74$

• $49 + 24 = 73$

• $13 + 29 = 42$

8 Ella is on a 452-mile road trip. She has driven 294 miles so far. Ella subtracts to find the number of miles she has left to drive. Her work is shown below.

Hundreds	Tens	Ones
	14	
	4̶	12
4	5̶	2̶
− 2	9	4
2	5	8

Part A

Explain Ella's mistake.

Part B

What is the correct answer?

Ella has _____ miles left to drive.

9 Circle the numbers that make each equation true.

$$541 - \boxed{\begin{matrix} 79 \\ 80 \\ 89 \end{matrix}} = 452 \qquad \boxed{\begin{matrix} 79 \\ 80 \\ 89 \end{matrix}} + 452 = 541$$

10 Select True or False for each equation.

A. $725 - 110 = 835$ ○ True   ○ False

B. $418 - 263 = 155$ ○ True   ○ False

C. $417 - 136 = 221$ ○ True   ○ False

D. $981 - 245 = 736$ ○ True   ○ False

11 Luke needs to solve the subtraction problem below. Which steps must he use? Mark all that apply.

$$625 - 473 = \boxed{}$$

○ **A.** Regroup 1 ten as 10 ones.

○ **B.** Subtract the ones: 5 ones − 3 ones.

○ **C.** Regroup 1 hundred as 10 tens.

○ **D.** Rename 2 tens as 12 tens.

○ **E.** Subtract the tens: 2 tens − 7 tens.

○ **F.** Subtract the hundreds: 6 hundreds − 4 hundreds.

○ **G.** Check the answer by adding 152 and 625.

Multiplying by Multiples of 10

1 GETTING THE IDEA

A **multiple** is the product of two numbers. A **multiple of 10** is the product of 10 and another number.

10×1	10×2	10×3	10×4	10×5	10×6
↓	↓	↓	↓	↓	↓

Multiples of 10: 10, 20, 30, 40, 50, 60, …

You can use models, place-value, properties of multiplication, and multiplication facts to multiply by multiples of 10.

Example 1

Cole bought 2 new shirts. Each shirt cost $30. How much did Cole spend on the two shirts?

Strategy   Use place-value models.

Step 1   Write the problem.

2 shirts for $30 each = 2×30

Step 2   Model the problem using place-value models.

2×30

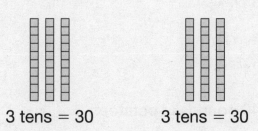

3 tens = 30   3 tens = 30

Step 3 ▸ Count the tens.

3 tens + 3 tens = 6 tens

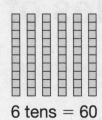

6 tens = 60

Solution Cole spent $60 on the two shirts.

Example 2

A restaurant bought 6 crates of potatoes. There are 40 pounds of potatoes in each crate. How many pounds of potatoes did the restaurant buy?

Strategy Use place value to multiply.

Step 1 ▸ Write the problem.

6 bags that are 40 pounds each = 6 × 40

Step 2 ▸ Use place value to rename the multiple of 10.

6 × **40** = 6 × **4 tens**

Step 3 ▸ Write the total number of tens.

Multiply 6 and 4 to find the total number of tens.

6 × 4 tens = **24** tens

Step 4 ▸ Regroup 10 tens as 1 hundred.

24 tens = 2 hundreds 4 tens

Step 5 ▸ Write the product in standard form.

2 hundreds 4 tens = 240

Solution The restaurant bought 240 pounds of potatoes.

You can also use properties of multiplication to find products.

The **commutative property of multiplication** says that changing the order of the factors does not change the product.

$$10 \times 5 = 50 \text{ or } 5 \times 10 = 50$$

The **associative property of multiplication** says that the factors can be grouped in different ways without changing the product.

$$2 \times 30 = 2 \times (3 \times 10)$$
$$= (2 \times 3) \times 10$$
$$= 6 \times 10$$
$$= 60$$

Example 3

Aaron runs for 60 minutes every day. How many minutes does he run in 3 days?

Strategy Use properties of multiplication to multiply.

Step 1 Write the problem.

3 days for 60 minutes each $= 3 \times 60$

Step 2 Write the multiple of 10 as a product of a number and 10.

$3 \times \mathbf{60} = 3 \times (\mathbf{6 \times 10})$

Step 3 Use the associative property of multiplication.

Group the factors a different way.

$3 \times 60 = 3 \times (6 \times 10)$
$= \mathbf{(3 \times 6)} \times 10$

Step 4 Multiply.

$3 \times 60 = \mathbf{(3 \times 6)} \times 10$ ⟵ Multiply 3 and 6.
$= \mathbf{18} \times 10$ ⟵ Multiply by 10.
$= 180$

Solution **Aaron runs for 180 minutes in 3 days.**

Example 4

Mrs. Turner buys 9 boxes of colored pencils. There are 30 colored pencils in each box. How many colored pencils did Mrs. Turner buy?

Strategy   Use a multiplication fact to multiply.

Step 1   Write the problem.

9 boxes of 30 pencils each = 9 × 30

Step 2   Think of a basic fact with 9 and 3.

9 × 3 = 27

Step 3   Use a pattern.

9 × 3 = 27

9 × 3**0** = 27**0**

Solution   Mrs. Turner bought 270 colored pencils.

There are 8 rows of seats in the theater. There are 20 seats in each row. How many seats are in the movie theater?

You can multiply _____ and _____ to find the total number of seats in the theater.

$8 \times 20 =$ _____ $\times ($ _____ $\times 10)$ Write the multiple of 10 as a product of a number and 10.

$= ($ _____ $\times$ _____ $) \times 10$ Use the _____ property of multiplication to group the factors a different way.

$=$ _____ $\times 10$ Multiply.

$=$ _____

There are _____ seats in the theater.

1 Which multiplication problem does the model represent?
Mark all that apply.

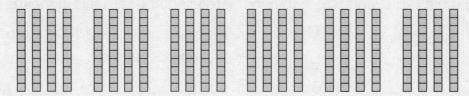

○ **A.** 6 × 30

○ **B.** 40 × 5

○ **C.** 30 × 6

○ **D.** 6 × 40

○ **E.** 5 × 40

○ **F.** 40 × 6

2 Ms. Ramone bought 5 video games. Each game costs $30.
How much did Ms. Ramone spend on those video games?

Make a model to solve the problem.

Ms. Ramone spent $ _____ on video games.

3 Select True or False for each number sentence.

A. 4 × 50 = 20   ○ True   ○ False

B. 7 × 70 = 490   ○ True   ○ False

C. 6 × 90 = 540   ○ True   ○ False

D. 8 × 60 = 420   ○ True   ○ False

4 Nina wants to plant 5 rows of 20 corn seeds. She used the multiplication problem 5×20 to find the number of seeds she will need. This is how Nina solved the problem:

$$5 \times 20 = 5 \times 2 \text{ tens} = 10 \text{ tens} = 1,000$$

Part A

What error did Nina make?

_____

Part B

Make a model to show the correct product.

Part C

Write the correct product.

$5 \times 20 = $ _____

5 A band practices 8 times before a concert. Each practice is 50 minutes long. How many total minutes will the band practice before the concert? Show your work.

The band will practice _____ total minutes before the concert.

6 Select a factor from each column to get the product of 240.

$$\begin{array}{|c|} \hline 2 \\ \hline 4 \\ \hline 6 \\ \hline \end{array} \times \begin{array}{|c|} \hline 30 \\ \hline 40 \\ \hline 50 \\ \hline \end{array} = 240$$

7 Pete and Julia are using building blocks to build towers.

- Pete makes 4 towers. He uses 20 blocks for each tower.

- Julia makes 2 towers. She uses 40 blocks for each tower.

Who used more blocks? Show your work.

8 Which has the same value as 7×90? Mark all that apply.

○ **A.** 6 hundreds 3 tens

○ **B.** $(7 \times 9) \times 10$

○ **C.** 63 tens

○ **D.** $(7 \times 10) \times (9 \times 10)$

○ **E.** 630 tens

○ **F.** 63×10

9 Zach has 4 boxes of crayons. There are 30 crayons in each box. How many total crayons does Zach have? Show your work.

10 Which multiplication fact would you use to solve each problem? Use numbers from the box to write the multiplication fact.

3×70

_____ × _____ = _____

9×30

_____ × _____ = _____

| 30 |
| 27 |
| 21 |
| 10 |
| 9 |
| 7 |
| 5 |
| 4 |
| 3 |

DOMAIN 2 REVIEW

1 What steps can be used to find the difference below? Mark all that apply.

714 − 168 = ☐

○ **A.** Subtract the ones: 8 ones − 4 ones.

○ **B.** Regroup 1 ten as 10 ones.

○ **C.** Regroup 1 hundred as 10 tens.

○ **D.** Rename 4 ones as 14 ones.

○ **E.** Subtract the tens: 11 tens − 6 tens.

○ **F.** Subtract the hundreds: 7 hundreds − 1 hundred.

○ **G.** Check the answer by adding 168 and 546.

2 Find the missing digits. Use the numbers from the box.

Hundreds	Tens	Ones
1	1	
2	☐	9
+ ☐	7	☐
9	1	3

2
3
4
5
6
7

3 Draw a line from each expanded form of a number to its standard form.

A. 30,000 + 30 + 3 •   • 30,303

B. 30,000 + 3,000 + 3 •   • 30,033

C. 30,000 + 3,000 + 30 •   • 33,003

D. 30,000 + 300 + 3 •   • 33,030

4 Jeb, Carmen, and River like taking walks in the morning.

- Jeb walks 20 minutes each day.
- Carmen walks 40 minutes each day.
- River walks 30 minutes each day.

Complete the table to find the total number of minutes each person walks in a week.

Person	Number of Days per Week	Total Number of Minutes
Jeb	7	
Carmen	5	
River	6	

Who walks the greatest number of minutes per week? _____

5 Circle the numbers that make the equation true.

	60	420
8 ×	70 =	640
	80	720

6 Read each statement about the number 29,486. Is the statement correct? Select Yes or No.

A. The digit 2 is in the thousands place. ○ Yes ○ No

B. The digit 8 has a value of 8. ○ Yes ○ No

C. The digit 4 has a value of 400. ○ Yes ○ No

D. The digit 9 is in the thousands place. ○ Yes ○ No

E. The digit 6 has a value of 6. ○ Yes ○ No

7 Select True or False for each equation.

A. $83 + 15 = 98$ ○ True ○ False

B. $37 + 78 = 105$ ○ True ○ False

C. $364 + 476 = 830$ ○ True ○ False

D. $513 + 291 = 804$ ○ True ○ False

E. $347 + 476 = 823$ ○ True ○ False

8 The nature center had 118 visitors on Friday. It had 421 total visitors on Friday and Saturday. How many visitors did the nature center have on Saturday? Show your work.

The nature center had _____ visitors on Saturday.

9 The table shows a number rounded to the nearest ten and nearest hundred. Use the numbers from the box to write the number that was rounded.

Number	Rounded to Nearest Ten	Rounded to Nearest Hundred
	650	700
	600	600
	650	600

595
615
644
648
653

10 Mr. Yates has an orange grove. There are about 1,000 orange trees in the grove when rounded to the nearest hundred. Mr. Yates said that the total number of trees in the grove is less than 1,000.

Part A

What is the possible number of orange trees in the grove? Explain your answer.

Part B

How many trees could be in the grove if there are about 950 trees when rounded to the nearest ten? Explain your answer.

Part C

Can all of the number of trees rounded to 950 also be rounded to 1,000? Explain.

11 James wrote the subtraction number sentence 984 − 798 = 196.

Maria used addition to check the problem. She said the difference is incorrect. What error did Maria find?

12 Derek used a place-value model to represent a number. Write the number in each of the forms below.

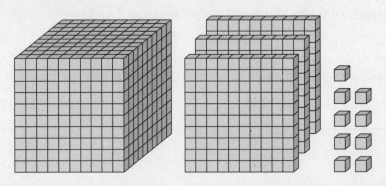

Standard form: _____

Expanded form: _____

Word form: _____

13 A zoo gift shop sold some stuffed animals.

Stuffed Animal	Number Sold
Bear	38
Gorilla	12
Lion	27

Rewrite the equation using an addition property to show an easy a way to find the total. Then find the total number of stuffed animals the zoo sold.

$38 + 12 + 27 =$ _____

$=$ _____

$=$ _____

_____ stuffed animals

Let's Walk!

You are participating in a Walk-A-Thon. People can make a donation of money or make a pledge to pay for each lap you walk around the track. The table shows the pledges and donations you have raised so far.

Pledges	Donations
$3 per lap	$8
$2 per lap	$9
	$12

Part A Your goal is to walk 4 laps. If you reach your goal, how much money will you raise from pledges made per lap? Show your work.

Part B How much money will you raise from donations? Show your work. Identify any properties of operations you use.

Part C What is the total amount you will raise in donations and pledges if you walk 4 laps around the track?

Part D Students earn prizes based on the total dollar amount they raised. The total amount is rounded up to the nearest 10 dollars to determine the prize.

Prize	Amount Raised
Super Bouncing Ball	$30
Yo-Yo	$40
Flashlight Pen	$50
Inflatable Chair	$60
2 Movie Tickets	$70

If you walked 4 laps, how much more money will you need to raise to earn the movie tickets? Tell the least amount of money you will need.

Part E Develop a plan for how you can raise enough money to earn the movie tickets. Show your work and explain your answer.

DOMAIN 3

Number and Operations – Fractions

Understanding Fractions

1 GETTING THE IDEA

A **fraction** is a number that names part of a whole.

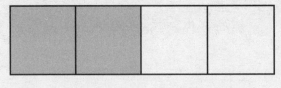

$\frac{2}{4}$ ← numerator
← denominator

The **numerator** is the top number. It tells how many equal parts are being considered.

The **denominator** is the bottom number. It tells how many equal parts there are in all.

You use fractions every day. You might eat $\frac{1}{4}$ of a sandwich. You practice piano for $\frac{1}{2}$ hour. You finish reading $\frac{1}{3}$ of a book. You live $\frac{7}{8}$ mile from school.

A **unit fraction** is 1 equal part of a whole. The numerator of a unit fraction is always 1.

1 out of 4 equal parts is shaded.

$\frac{1}{4}$, or one fourth

Example 1
What unit fraction names the shaded part of the figure?

Strategy   Find the number of shaded parts and equal parts.

Step 1   Write the numerator of the fraction.

There is 1 shaded part.
The numerator of all unit fractions is 1.
Write 1 in the numerator.

Step 2   Write the denominator of the fraction.

There are 3 equal parts in the whole.
Write 3 in the denominator.

Solution   The shaded part of the figure shows $\frac{1}{3}$.

Example 2

Which drawing shows $\frac{1}{6}$? Mark all that apply.

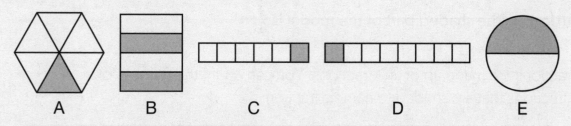

A   B   C   D   E

Strategy   Find a drawing divided into sixths with 1 part shaded.

Step 1   Find the drawings that show sixths.

A and C have 6 equal parts. They show sixths.

B, D, and E have 4, 8, and 2 equal parts.

Step 2   Of the drawing showing sixths, find the drawings with only 1 equal part shaded.

A and C both have only 1 equal part shaded.

Solution   Drawings A and C both show $\frac{1}{6}$.

Example 3

What fraction names the shaded part of the model?

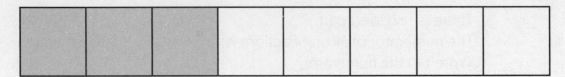

Strategy   Find the numerator and denominator of the fraction.

Step 1   Count the number of equal parts in all.

There are 8 equal parts in the whole.
The denominator is 8.

Step 2   Count the number of parts that are shaded.

Three of the parts are shaded. The numerator is 3.

Solution   The shaded part of the model is $\frac{3}{8}$.

All fractions are made up of unit fractions. You can count the number of unit fractions that are shaded to name a fraction.

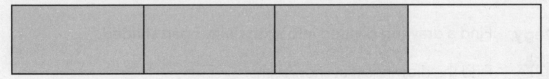

Each equal part shows $\frac{1}{4}$.

Three $\frac{1}{4}$-size parts are shaded.

$\frac{3}{4}$ of the whole is shaded.

Example 4

What fraction names the shaded part?

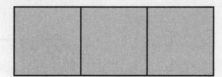

Strategy Count the number of unit fractions that are shaded.

Step 1 Identify the unit fraction.

There are 3 equal parts, so each equal part shows $\frac{1}{3}$.

Step 2 Count the number of unit fractions that are shaded.

Three $\frac{1}{3}$-size parts are shaded.

Solution The shaded part is $\frac{3}{3}$.

2 COACHED EXAMPLE

Make a model to show the fraction $\frac{2}{3}$. Use the rectangle below.

The denominator is _____.

Divide the rectangle into _____ equal parts.

Each equal part shows the unit fraction _____.

Shade _____ equal parts.

1 Which drawing shows a unit fraction? Mark all that apply.

○ A.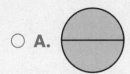

○ D.

○ B.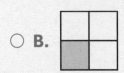

○ E.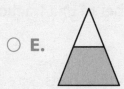

○ C.

○ F.

2 The students in Mr. Henry's class were discussing the fraction $\frac{2}{8}$. Select True or False for each statement.

A. It has eight $\frac{1}{2}$-size parts. ○ True ○ False

B. It has two $\frac{1}{8}$-size parts. ○ True ○ False

C. A drawing would show 8 equal parts with 8 parts shaded. ○ True ○ False

D. A drawing would show 8 equal parts with 2 parts shaded. ○ True ○ False

E. It has a numerator of 1 and a denominator of 8. ○ True ○ False

3 Draw a line from each drawing to the fraction that names it.

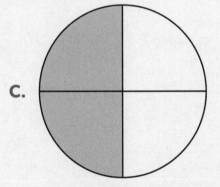

A.

B.

C.

D.

•

•

•

•

•

•

•

•

$\dfrac{3}{6}$

$\dfrac{5}{8}$

$\dfrac{2}{3}$

$\dfrac{2}{4}$

4 Circle the fraction that makes the statement true.

The shaded part of 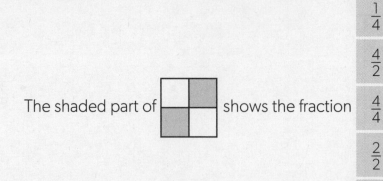 shows the fraction

$$\frac{1}{4}$$

$$\frac{4}{2}$$

$$\frac{4}{4}$$

$$\frac{2}{2}$$

$$\frac{2}{4}$$

5 Is the fraction a unit fraction? Select Yes or No.

A. $\frac{4}{6}$ ○ Yes ○ No

B. $\frac{1}{3}$ ○ Yes ○ No

C. $\frac{2}{2}$ ○ Yes ○ No

D. $\frac{1}{8}$ ○ Yes ○ No

E. $\frac{2}{1}$ ○ Yes ○ No

6 Use the grid below to make a drawing that shows $\frac{5}{6}$.

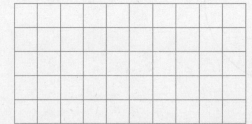

7 Use the numbers in the box to complete the statements about the drawing.

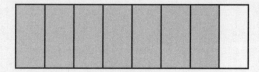

The drawing shows the fraction _____.

There are _____ equal parts in all, with _____ parts shaded.

There are _____ unit fractions that are shaded, and each part represents the unit fraction _____.

8
7
3
1
$\frac{7}{8}$
$\frac{1}{8}$

8 Parker is looking for a model that shows $\frac{6}{8}$. Which model could Parker select? Mark all that apply.

○ **A.**

○ **B.**

○ **C.**

○ **D.**

9 Look at the fractions. Write the fraction in the correct box.

$\frac{2}{2}$ $\frac{1}{3}$ $\frac{5}{6}$ $\frac{1}{4}$ $\frac{7}{8}$ $\frac{1}{6}$ $\frac{1}{8}$

Unit Fractions	Not Unit Fractions

10 Write the fraction that the drawing shows. Explain your answer.

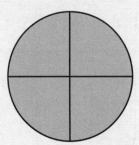

3.NF.2.a, 3.NF.2.b

Fractions on a Number Line

You can use a number line to model fractions. This number line shows one whole as the length between 0 and 1.

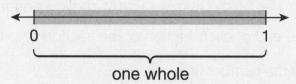

One whole can be divided into equal parts, or fractions.

Example 1

Luis cut a plank of wood into three equal pieces. Each piece is $\frac{1}{3}$ of the whole plank. Show $\frac{1}{3}$ on a number line.

Strategy   Use fraction strips to mark equal parts on a number line.

  Step 1   Draw a number line.

            Match the length from 0 to 1 to a fraction strip.

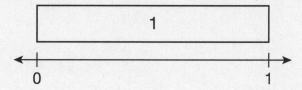

Step 2 ▶ Divide the number line into equal parts.

Use fraction strips that show thirds.
Each strip is the same length, so each section on the number line will have the same value.

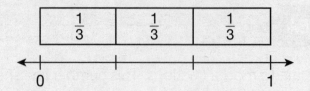

Draw marks on the number line to show 3 equal parts.

Use the end of each section of the fraction strip to place the marks.

Step 3 ▶ Show $\frac{1}{3}$ on the number line.

Ring the length from 0 to $\frac{1}{3}$.

Write the fraction name for that length at the mark.

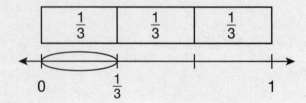

$\frac{1}{3}$ numerator ← the number of equal parts ringed
denominator ← the total number of equal parts in a whole

Solution The number line in Step 3 shows $\frac{1}{3}$.

Example 2

Show $\frac{3}{4}$ on the number line.

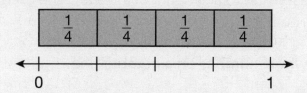

Strategy Ring equal parts on a number line until you get to $\frac{3}{4}$.

Step 1 Start at 0. Ring the first equal part.

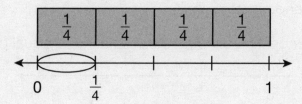

$\frac{1}{4}$ numerator ← the number of equal parts ringed
denominator ← the total number of equal parts in a whole

There is one part of $\frac{1}{4}$.

Step 2 Ring the second and third equal parts.

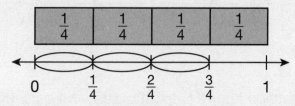

$\frac{3}{4}$ numerator ← the number of equal parts ringed
denominator ← the total number of equal parts in a whole

There are three parts of $\frac{1}{4}$.

Solution The number line in Step 2 shows $\frac{3}{4}$.

Example 3

Meg cut a straw into fourths. She used the entire straw in an art project.
Write a fraction to represent the total amount of the straw she used.
Show your answer on a number line.

Strategy   Model a whole number on a number line.

Step 1   Find the denominator.

Meg cut the straw into fourths.

There are 4 equal parts in the whole straw.

The denominator is 4.

Step 2   Mark a number line dividing the whole into 4 equal parts.

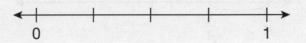

Step 3   Ring fraction parts.

Meg used 4 pieces. Ring 4 parts.

Label the lengths with fractions.

Step 4   Write the fraction for the amount of straw Meg used.

$\dfrac{4}{4}$ numerator $\longleftarrow$ the number of equal parts used
     denominator $\longleftarrow$ the total number of equal parts in a whole

$\dfrac{4}{4}$ has the same value as 1 whole.

$\dfrac{4}{4} = 1$

Solution   Meg used $\dfrac{4}{4}$ of a whole straw. The number line in Step 3 shows $\dfrac{4}{4}$.

Example 4

Show $\frac{3}{2}$ on the number line.

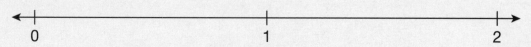

Strategy   Show wholes divided into equal parts.

Step 1   Determine how many equal parts you need.

The fraction $\frac{3}{2}$ has 2 as the denominator.

You need to show halves on the number line.

Step 2   Divide each whole into 2 equal parts.

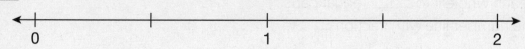

Step 3   Ring fraction parts.

You want to show $\frac{3}{2}$, or three halves, so ring 3 parts.

Label the lengths with fractions.

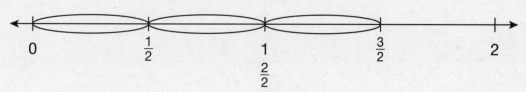

Solution   The number line in Step 3 shows $\frac{3}{2}$.

Show $\frac{5}{3}$ on the number line.

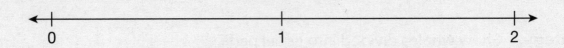

The fraction $\frac{5}{3}$ has _____ as the denominator.

Divide each whole into _____ equal parts.
Label the number line with fractions.

Ring _____ parts on the number line to show $\frac{5}{3}$.

The length marked on the number line shows _____.

1 Jorge wants to show $\frac{1}{2}$ on the number line. Mark the number line to show halves. Write the fraction $\frac{1}{2}$ in the correct place.

2 Draw a line from each number line to the fraction it shows.

A.  • • $\frac{3}{2}$

B. • • $\frac{2}{3}$

C. • • $\frac{3}{4}$

D. • • $\frac{8}{6}$

3 Label and ring the number line below to show $\frac{5}{8}$. Explain how you found the fraction. Use words or numbers to explain.

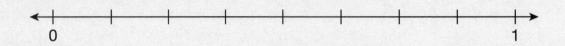

0   1

(blank answer box)

4 Reg divided a rope into fourths. He showed his work on the number line below. Reg used three of the rope parts to make a basket. Use the numbers in the box to complete each statement.

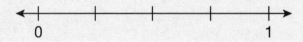

0   1

Reg divided his rope into _____ equal parts.

Each section of rope is _____ of the whole rope.

Reg used _____ of the whole rope.

3

4

$\frac{1}{4}$

$\frac{3}{4}$

$\frac{4}{4}$

5 Ana cut a board into sixths. She used all of the pieces to make a border around her plant.

Part A

Divide the number line into six equal parts. Write the fraction of the board Ana used in the box provided.

0   1

Part B

How many pieces of board did Ana use? _____

Part C

What whole number is equal to the fraction of wood board that Ana used? _____

6 The number line below shows two wholes, each divided into the same number of equal parts. Circle the number that makes each statement true.

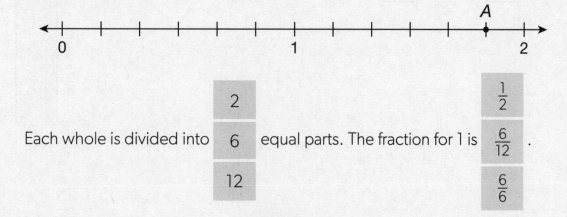

Each whole is divided into
$\boxed{2}$ $\boxed{6}$ $\boxed{12}$
equal parts. The fraction for 1 is
$\boxed{\dfrac{1}{2}}$ $\boxed{\dfrac{6}{12}}$ $\boxed{\dfrac{6}{6}}$.

The letter A is above the fraction
$\boxed{\dfrac{5}{6}}$ $\boxed{\dfrac{11}{12}}$ $\boxed{\dfrac{11}{6}}$.

7 Pam had 2 equal strings. She cut each string into eighths. She used 9 of the parts. Use the number line below. Divide each whole into 8 equal parts. Mark the number line to show eighths. Label $\frac{9}{8}$.

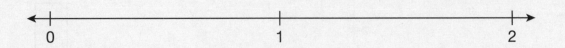

8 Use fractions from the box to label the number line.

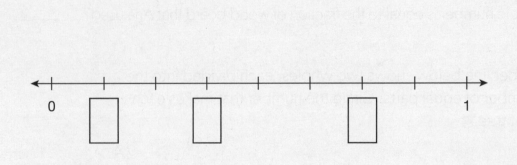

$\frac{1}{7}$

$\frac{1}{8}$

$\frac{3}{5}$

$\frac{3}{8}$

$\frac{6}{2}$

$\frac{6}{8}$

$\frac{7}{8}$

Equivalent Fractions

1 GETTING THE IDEA

Equivalent fractions are fractions that have different numerators and denominators but name the same part or amount.

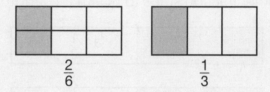

$\frac{2}{6}$

$\frac{1}{3}$

$\frac{2}{6}$ and $\frac{1}{3}$ are equivalent fractions because they name the same part of a whole. Their numerators and denominators are different because there are a different number of equal-sized parts.

You can use an equal sign to show that two fractions are equivalent.

$$\frac{2}{6} = \frac{1}{3}$$

Example 1
Write two fractions equivalent to $\frac{1}{2}$.

$\frac{1}{2}$	$\frac{1}{2}$

$\frac{1}{4}$	$\frac{1}{4}$	$\frac{1}{4}$	$\frac{1}{4}$

$\frac{1}{8}$	$\frac{1}{8}$	$\frac{1}{8}$	$\frac{1}{8}$	$\frac{1}{8}$	$\frac{1}{8}$	$\frac{1}{8}$	$\frac{1}{8}$

Strategy   Use fraction strips.

Step 1   Shade $\frac{1}{2}$ of the fraction strip that shows halves.

$\frac{1}{2}$	$\frac{1}{2}$

$\frac{1}{4}$	$\frac{1}{4}$	$\frac{1}{4}$	$\frac{1}{4}$

$\frac{1}{8}$	$\frac{1}{8}$	$\frac{1}{8}$	$\frac{1}{8}$	$\frac{1}{8}$	$\frac{1}{8}$	$\frac{1}{8}$	$\frac{1}{8}$

Step 2   Shade the other fraction strips to match the length of $\frac{1}{2}$.

$\frac{1}{2}$	$\frac{1}{2}$

$\frac{1}{4}$	$\frac{1}{4}$	$\frac{1}{4}$	$\frac{1}{4}$

$\frac{1}{8}$	$\frac{1}{8}$	$\frac{1}{8}$	$\frac{1}{8}$	$\frac{1}{8}$	$\frac{1}{8}$	$\frac{1}{8}$	$\frac{1}{8}$

The same part of each fraction strip is shaded.
So, the strips show equivalent fractions.

Step 3   Write fractions that describe the shaded parts of the fraction strips.

$$\frac{1}{4} + \frac{1}{4} = \frac{2}{4}$$

$$\frac{1}{8} + \frac{1}{8} + \frac{1}{8} + \frac{1}{8} = \frac{4}{8}$$

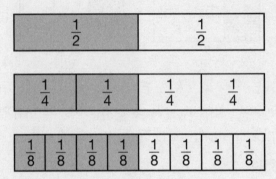

Solution   Two fractions equivalent to $\frac{1}{2}$ are $\frac{2}{4}$ and $\frac{4}{8}$.

Example 2

Find the missing numerator.

$$\frac{2}{3} = \frac{\boxed{}}{6}$$

Strategy   **Draw a model.**

Step 1   Draw a model to show $\frac{2}{3}$.

Step 2   Divide the parts of the model to show sixths.

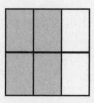

Step 3   Count the number of sixths that are shaded.

4 out of 6 equal parts are shaded.

$\frac{4}{6}$ of the model is shaded.

$$\frac{2}{3} = \frac{4}{6}$$

Solution   **The missing numerator is 4.**

Example 3

Draw a line from each fraction to an equivalent fraction.

A. $\frac{3}{4}$ •   • $\frac{4}{8}$

B. $\frac{1}{3}$ •   • $\frac{6}{8}$

C. $\frac{3}{6}$ •   • $\frac{4}{6}$

D. $\frac{2}{3}$ •   • $\frac{2}{6}$

Strategy   Use fraction strips.

Step 1   Use fraction strips to model each fraction.

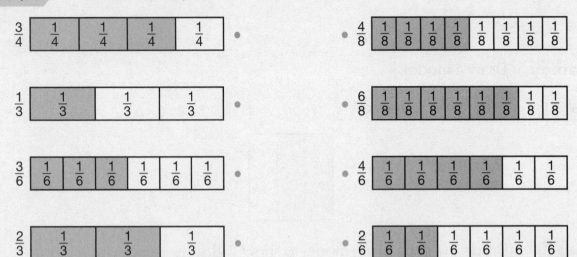

Step 2   Match the fraction strips that show equal shaded parts.

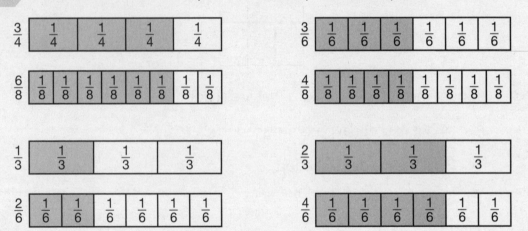

Step 3   Draw lines to match the equivalent fractions.

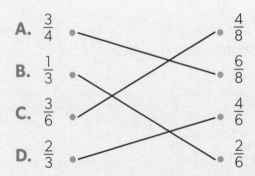

A. $\frac{3}{4}$

B. $\frac{1}{3}$

C. $\frac{3}{6}$

D. $\frac{2}{3}$

$\frac{4}{8}$

$\frac{6}{8}$

$\frac{4}{6}$

$\frac{2}{6}$

Solution   Equivalent fractions are shown in Step 3.

You can also use number lines to determine if fractions are equivalent.

Two fractions are equivalent if they are at the same point on a number line.

Example 4

Are $\frac{1}{4}$ and $\frac{2}{8}$ equivalent fractions?

Strategy   Use a number line.

Step 1   Draw a number line that shows fourths.

Mark the point for $\frac{1}{4}$.

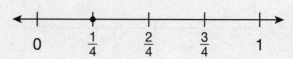

Step 2   Draw tick marks to show eighths on the same number line.

Label the eighths.

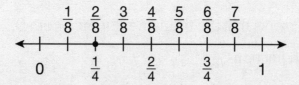

Step 3   Find $\frac{2}{8}$ on the number line. Compare its location to $\frac{1}{4}$.

The fractions $\frac{2}{8}$ and $\frac{1}{4}$ are at the same place on the number line.

Solution $\frac{1}{4}$ and $\frac{2}{8}$ are equivalent fractions.

Use the number lines to write three equivalent fractions.

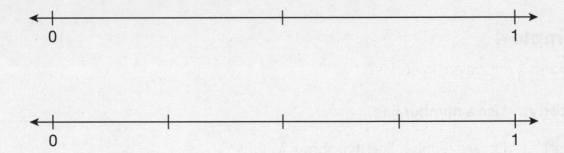

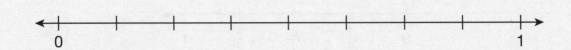

Draw points on the tick marks that are the same distance from 0.

Label the tick marks with fractions.

Points at the same spot on the number line are for _____, _____, and _____.

The fractions _____, _____, and _____ are equivalent.

1 Is each fraction equivalent to $\frac{2}{4}$? Select Yes or No.

$\frac{1}{2}$	$\frac{1}{2}$

$\frac{1}{3}$	$\frac{1}{3}$	$\frac{1}{3}$

$\frac{1}{4}$	$\frac{1}{4}$	$\frac{1}{4}$	$\frac{1}{4}$

$\frac{1}{6}$	$\frac{1}{6}$	$\frac{1}{6}$	$\frac{1}{6}$	$\frac{1}{6}$	$\frac{1}{6}$

$\frac{1}{8}$	$\frac{1}{8}$	$\frac{1}{8}$	$\frac{1}{8}$	$\frac{1}{8}$	$\frac{1}{8}$	$\frac{1}{8}$	$\frac{1}{8}$

A. $\frac{4}{8}$ ○ Yes ○ No

B. $\frac{2}{3}$ ○ Yes ○ No

C. $\frac{3}{6}$ ○ Yes ○ No

D. $\frac{2}{8}$ ○ Yes ○ No

E. $\frac{3}{4}$ ○ Yes ○ No

F. $\frac{1}{2}$ ○ Yes ○ No

2 Draw a line from each fraction to an equivalent fraction.

A. $\frac{1}{2}$ •   • $\frac{4}{6}$

B. $\frac{2}{6}$ •   • $\frac{4}{8}$

C. $\frac{2}{3}$ •   • $\frac{2}{8}$

D. $\frac{1}{4}$ •   • $\frac{3}{4}$

E. $\frac{6}{8}$ •   • $\frac{1}{3}$

3 Mrs. Ortez wrote these fractions on the board for her class.

$$\frac{2}{3} \quad \frac{4}{6}$$

Select True or False for each statement about the fractions.

A. The numerators and denominators of the fractions are different, so the fractions are not equivalent.   ○ True   ○ False

B. The fractions name the same part of a whole.   ○ True   ○ False

C. Because 3 is less than 6, thirds are smaller than sixths.   ○ True   ○ False

D. The fraction $\frac{2}{3}$ describes 2 parts and $\frac{4}{6}$ describes 4 parts, so $\frac{2}{3}$ and $\frac{4}{6}$ cannot be equivalent fractions.   ○ True   ○ False

E. The fractions are equivalent fractions.   ○ True   ○ False

4 Which number sentence could this number line be used to model? Mark all that apply.

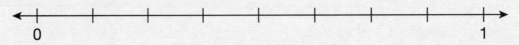

0   1

○ **A.** $\frac{4}{8} = \frac{2}{3}$

○ **B.** $\frac{2}{4} = \frac{1}{2}$

○ **C.** $\frac{1}{2} = \frac{3}{6}$

○ **D.** $\frac{3}{4} = \frac{6}{8}$

○ **E.** $\frac{1}{2} = \frac{4}{8}$

5 Use numbers from the box to complete the equivalent fractions.

$$\frac{4}{8} = \frac{\boxed{}}{4}$$

$$\frac{2}{3} = \frac{4}{\boxed{}}$$

$$\frac{3}{6} = \frac{\boxed{}}{2}$$

$$\frac{1}{2} = \frac{4}{\boxed{}}$$

| 1 |
| 2 |
| 3 |
| 4 |
| 6 |
| 8 |

6 The shaded part of this sandwich is the part that Hank ate.

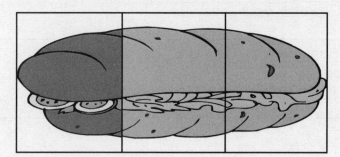

Compare each fraction to the part Hank ate. Write the fraction in the correct box.

| $\frac{2}{3}$ | $\frac{4}{8}$ | $\frac{1}{3}$ | $\frac{1}{2}$ | $\frac{4}{6}$ | $\frac{2}{6}$ |

Part Hank Ate	Part Left Over	Neither

7 Mr. Craft wrote this problem on the board.

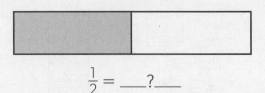

$$\frac{1}{2} = \underline{\quad}?\underline{\quad}$$

He asked his students to use the model to write a fraction that is equivalent to $\frac{1}{2}$. The work of two students is shown.

Todd's Work	Gabriella's Work
$\frac{1}{2} = \frac{3}{4}$	$\frac{1}{2} = \frac{3}{6}$

Who is correct? Explain your answer.

8 Three friends, Marcy, Dan, and Rose, all made pizzas that are the same size.

- Marcy cut her pizza into 6 equal slices. She ate 4 of the pieces.
- Dan cut his pizza into 8 equal slices. He ate 3 of the slices.
- Rose cut her pizza into 3 equal slices. She ate 2 of the slices.

Which friends ate the same amount of pizza? _____

Use words, numbers, or pictures to explain how you know your answer is correct.

Whole Numbers as Fractions

1 GETTING THE IDEA

A whole number can be written as an **equivalent fraction**. When the numerator and denominator are the same, they name the whole number 1.

1 whole

$1 = \frac{2}{2}$

$1 = \frac{4}{4}$

Remember:

$\frac{4}{4}$ ← The numerator tells how many equal parts are shaded or counted.
  ← The denominator tells how many equal parts are in the whole.

Whole numbers other than 1 can also be written as fractions. For example:

4 wholes $4 = \frac{4}{1}$

3 wholes $3 = \frac{3}{1}$

When the numerator is a whole number greater than 1 and the denominator is 1, the fraction names a whole number greater than 1.

Example 1

Which of the fractions below name a whole number?

$$\frac{2}{1}, \frac{3}{2}, \frac{1}{3}, \frac{3}{3}, \frac{3}{2}, \frac{6}{1}, \frac{6}{6}$$

Strategy   Find the fractions that are equal to 1. Find fractions that have 1 as a denominator.

Step 1   Find fractions with the same numerator and denominator.
These fractions are equal to 1.

$$\frac{3}{3} = 1 \qquad \frac{6}{6} = 1$$

Step 2   Find fractions with denominators of 1.
These fractions are whole numbers.

$$\frac{2}{1} = 2 \qquad \frac{6}{1} = 6$$

Solution $\frac{3}{3}, \frac{6}{6}, \frac{2}{1}$, and $\frac{6}{1}$ name whole numbers.

Remember that any whole number can be represented as a fraction. Simply place the number as a numerator over a denominator of 1.

Example 2

What fraction and whole number does the model show?

Strategy   Count the number of parts and the number of wholes.

Step 1   Name the number of wholes.

There are 3 wholes.

Step 2   Name the number of parts in each whole.

There is one part in each whole.

Step 3   Name the numerator and denominator.

$$\frac{3}{1} \quad \begin{array}{l} \leftarrow 3 \text{ wholes} \\ \leftarrow 1 \text{ part in the whole} \end{array}$$

Solution   The drawing shows $\frac{3}{1}$, or 3.

Example 3

Use the number line to find fractions and whole numbers that are equivalent.

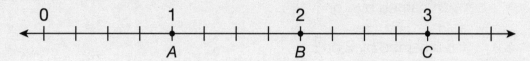

Strategy   **Count to a whole number on the number line, and label it with an equivalent fraction.**

Step 1   Find how many equal parts are in each whole.

Each whole is divided into 4 equal parts.

Step 2   Count by fourths to find the value of A. Label the number line.

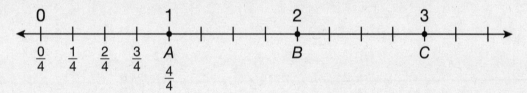

The value of A is $\frac{4}{4}$.

Step 3   Continue counting by fourths, and label the value of B.

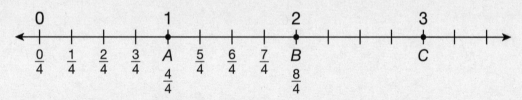

The value of B is $\frac{8}{4}$.

Step 4   Continue counting by fourths and label the value of C.

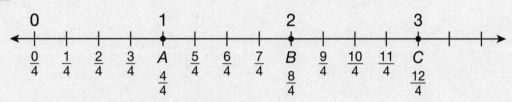

The value of C is $\frac{12}{4}$.

Step 5   Identify the points on the number line that can be named by both a whole number and a fraction.

     A is named by 1 or $\frac{4}{4}$.

     B is named by 2 or $\frac{8}{4}$.

     C is named by 3 or $\frac{12}{4}$.

Solution   The number line shows that $\frac{4}{4} = 1$, $\frac{8}{4} = 2$, and $\frac{12}{4} = 3$.

Write the fraction for each model.

Look at the model on the left. There are _____ whole figures there.

Is each figure divided into parts? _____

There is _____ part in each whole figure.

Write the fraction.

The number of whole figures is the _____.

The number of parts in each figure is the _____.

So the fraction for the model on the left is _____.

Look at the model on the right. There is _____ whole figure there.

Is the figure divided into parts? _____

There are _____ equal parts in the figure.

There are _____ shaded parts.

Write the fraction.

The number of shaded parts is the _____.

The number of equal parts is the _____.

So the fraction for the model on the right is _____.

The fractions for the models are _____ and _____.

1 Write three fractions that name whole numbers greater than 1.

_____   _____   _____

2 Does the fraction name a whole number or not? Write the fraction in the correct box.

| $\frac{4}{1}$ | $\frac{1}{3}$ | $\frac{6}{6}$ | $\frac{2}{4}$ | $\frac{8}{1}$ | $\frac{4}{4}$ | $\frac{1}{8}$ | $\frac{4}{1}$ |

Whole Number	Not a Whole Number

3 Which statement describes the fraction $\frac{2}{1}$ correctly? Mark all that apply.

○ **A.** It is equivalent to the whole number 1.

○ **B.** It is equivalent to the whole number 2.

○ **C.** It is equivalent to $\frac{1}{2}$.

○ **D.** It is at the same point as $\frac{1}{2}$ on a number line.

○ **E.** It is at the point 2 on a number line.

4 Circle the numbers that make the statement true about the model below.

The model shows the fraction
$\frac{1}{1}$
$\frac{2}{2}$
$\frac{1}{2}$, which is equivalent to
$\frac{2}{1}$
$\frac{4}{1}$

3
2
1 .
4
5

5 Does the fraction name a whole number? Select Yes or No.

A. $\frac{5}{1}$ ○ Yes ○ No

B. $\frac{6}{1}$ ○ Yes ○ No

C. $\frac{1}{6}$ ○ Yes ○ No

D. $\frac{1}{3}$ ○ Yes ○ No

E. $\frac{9}{1}$ ○ Yes ○ No

6 Select True or False for each statement.

A. 16 and $\frac{16}{1}$ name the same number.   ○ True ○ False

B. $\frac{3}{6}$ is equivalent to a whole number.   ○ True ○ False

C. $\frac{5}{5}$ and $\frac{5}{1}$ name the same point on a number line.   ○ True ○ False

D. $\frac{8}{8}$ and $\frac{6}{6}$ name the same whole number.   ○ True ○ False

E. 4 and $\frac{1}{4}$ are equivalent.   ○ True ○ False

7 Draw a line from each fraction to its equivalent whole number.

A. $\frac{2}{1}$ •   • 8

B. $\frac{6}{6}$ •   • 10

C. $\frac{10}{1}$ •   • 2

D. $\frac{8}{1}$ •   • 1

8 Mike says that both fractions, $\frac{6}{1}$ and $\frac{6}{6}$, are equivalent to the whole number 6. Do you agree? Use drawings, words, or symbols to explain your answer.

9 Lucas mowed $\frac{3}{3}$ of his lawn.

Part A

Draw a picture to show the part he mowed.

Part B

Complete the number sentence below.

$\frac{3}{3} =$ _____

Part C

Did Lucas mow his whole lawn? Explain your answer.

10 Use the number line below.

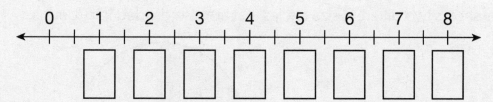

Part A

Write the fractions that represent the whole numbers on the number line.

Part B

Explain the relationship between the whole numbers and the fractions you wrote.

Comparing Fractions

1 GETTING THE IDEA

You can compare fractions that refer to either the same-size whole or the same-size group.

This model shows two same-size circles that are each divided into fourths.

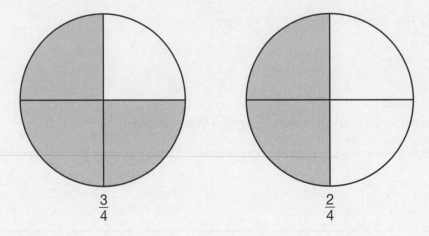

The parts are of equal size. The model shows that 3 of the same-size parts are greater than 2. So, $\frac{3}{4}$ is greater than $\frac{2}{4}$.

This model shows two different-size circles that are also divided into fourths.

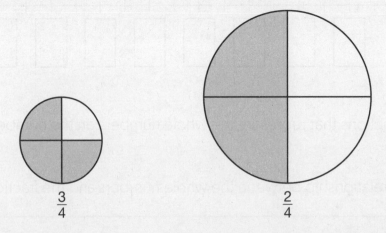

The circles are different sizes, so the fourths are different sizes. You cannot compare the fractions because the wholes are different.

When you compare fractions, you use the same symbols you use with whole numbers.

> **is greater than**

< **is less than**

= **is equal to**

When you compare fractions that have the same denominator, the size of the numerator determines which fraction is greater.

Example 1

Compare $\frac{2}{6}$ and $\frac{5}{6}$. Use >, <, or =.

Strategy **The denominators are the same. Compare the numerators.**

Step 1 Compare the numerators.

$2 < 5$, so $\frac{2}{6} < \frac{5}{6}$.

Step 2 Draw a number line to check your answer.

Label points on the number line to represent $\frac{2}{6}$ and $\frac{5}{6}$.

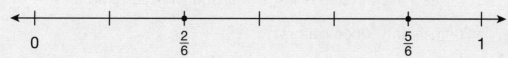

Step 3 Compare the locations of the points on the number line.

Since $\frac{2}{6}$ is closer to 0 than $\frac{5}{6}$, $\frac{2}{6}$ is less than $\frac{5}{6}$.

Solution $\frac{2}{6} < \frac{5}{6}$, or $\frac{5}{6} > \frac{2}{6}$

When you compare fractions that have the same numerator, you are comparing the same number of parts of a whole. The difference is the size of the parts. So you compare the denominators, which tell the sizes of the parts.

Example 2

Compare $\frac{3}{4}$ and $\frac{3}{8}$. Use $>$, $<$, or $=$.

Strategy   **The numerators are the same. Compare the denominators.**

Step 1   Use fraction strips to model the problem.

Show $\frac{3}{4}$ and $\frac{3}{8}$.

$\frac{1}{4}$	$\frac{1}{4}$	$\frac{1}{4}$	$\frac{1}{4}$

$\frac{1}{8}$	$\frac{1}{8}$	$\frac{1}{8}$	$\frac{1}{8}$	$\frac{1}{8}$	$\frac{1}{8}$	$\frac{1}{8}$	$\frac{1}{8}$

Step 2   Compare the lengths of the fraction strips.

The $\frac{3}{4}$ fraction strip is longer than the $\frac{3}{8}$ fraction strip.

Step 3   Compare the denominators.

The fewer parts that a whole is divided into, the larger the parts.

Fourths are larger than eighths, so the fraction 3 fourths is greater than 3 eighths.

$$\frac{3}{4} > \frac{3}{8}$$

Solution $\frac{3}{4} > \frac{3}{8}$, or $\frac{3}{8} < \frac{3}{4}$

Example 3

Angie and Toya have the same amount of math homework to do. Angie finished $\frac{1}{6}$ of her math homework. Toya finished $\frac{1}{3}$ of her math homework. Who has finished the greater amount of homework?

Strategy   Use reasoning.

Step 1   Identify what the problem asks you to compare.

Compare the part of her homework that Angie finished to the part that Toya finished.

Step 2   The numerators are the same. Compare denominators.

The denominator 6 shows that 1 whole is divided into 6 same-size parts.

The denominator 3 shows that 1 whole is divided into 3 same-size parts.

The more parts that a whole is divided into, the smaller the parts.

Sixths are smaller than thirds. 1 sixth is smaller than 1 third.

$$\frac{1}{6} < \frac{1}{3}$$

Step 3   Look back at the problem, and answer the question.

The problem asks who finished the greater amount of homework.

Angie finished $\frac{1}{6}$ of her homework. Toya finished $\frac{1}{3}$ of her homework. Because $\frac{1}{3}$ is greater than $\frac{1}{6}$, Toya finished the greater amount of homework.

Solution   **Toya finished the greater amount of homework.**

Last week, Landon's bean plant grew $\frac{2}{6}$ foot. Tyrell's bean plant grew $\frac{2}{8}$ foot. Whose plant grew more last week? Check your answer.

Look at the fractions.

$\frac{2}{6}$ and $\frac{2}{8}$ have the same _____.

You should compare the _____.

The _____ is the number of parts a whole is divided into, so if

the number of parts is greater, the parts are _____.

So, sixths are _____ than eighths.

$$\frac{\boxed{}}{\boxed{}} > \frac{\boxed{}}{\boxed{}}$$

Draw a model to check your answer.

_____ plant grew more last week.

1 Is the fraction greater than $\frac{3}{8}$? Select Yes or No.

A. $\frac{2}{8}$ ○ Yes ○ No

B. $\frac{3}{4}$ ○ Yes ○ No

C. $\frac{3}{8}$ ○ Yes ○ No

D. $\frac{3}{6}$ ○ Yes ○ No

E. $\frac{7}{8}$ ○ Yes ○ No

2 Lily walked less than $\frac{2}{4}$ mile to the park. How far could she have walked? Mark all that apply.

○ A. $\frac{2}{6}$ mile   ○ D. $\frac{2}{3}$ mile

○ B. $\frac{1}{4}$ mile   ○ E. $\frac{3}{4}$ mile

○ C. $\frac{2}{4}$ mile   ○ F. $\frac{2}{8}$ mile

3 Compare each fraction to $\frac{3}{6}$. Write the fraction in the correct box.

| $\frac{5}{6}$ | $\frac{3}{8}$ | $\frac{1}{6}$ | $\frac{3}{4}$ | $\frac{4}{6}$ |

Less Than $\frac{3}{6}$	Greater Than $\frac{3}{6}$

4 Brady wrote a number sentence that correctly compares fractions. Which sentence could he have written? Mark all that apply.

○ **A.** $\frac{6}{8} > \frac{4}{8}$ ○ **D.** $\frac{2}{6} > \frac{2}{3}$

○ **B.** $\frac{4}{6} = \frac{2}{3}$ ○ **E.** $\frac{4}{6} > \frac{4}{8}$

○ **C.** $\frac{3}{8} < \frac{3}{4}$ ○ **F.** $\frac{5}{8} < \frac{2}{8}$

5 Mr. Adams wrote the fractions below on the board.

$\frac{6}{8}$ $\frac{3}{8}$

Part A

Write two number sentences that compare the fractions.
Use the symbols >, <, or =.

_____

_____

Part B

Draw a model to check the sentences you wrote.

6 Use numbers from the box to complete the number sentences.
Use each number only once.

3
4
6
8

7 Select True or False for each sentence.

A. $\frac{7}{8} > \frac{5}{8}$ ○ True ○ False

B. $\frac{1}{6} = \frac{1}{6}$ ○ True ○ False

C. $\frac{2}{3} < \frac{2}{4}$ ○ True ○ False

D. $\frac{4}{6} > \frac{5}{6}$ ○ True ○ False

E. $\frac{2}{6} < \frac{2}{4}$ ○ True ○ False

F. $\frac{1}{2} = \frac{1}{8}$ ○ True ○ False

8 Melia ate $\frac{2}{4}$ of a sub for lunch. Carrie ate $\frac{2}{6}$ of the same size sub for lunch.

- Melia said that she ate more because $\frac{2}{4} > \frac{2}{6}$.

- Carrie said that she ate more because $\frac{2}{4} < \frac{2}{6}$.

Who is correct? _____

What error could the other person have made?

9 All of the students in Ms. Reel's class are reading the same book. Maddie has read $\frac{2}{3}$ of the book. Anna has read $\frac{2}{8}$ of the book.

Who has more of the book left to read? _____ Explain.

10 The table shows the distances that three children live from the school they all attend.

Children	Distance from School (in miles)
Demetri	$\frac{3}{8}$
Angelo	$\frac{5}{6}$
Edgar	$\frac{5}{8}$

Part A

Compare the fractions of a mile that have the same denominator.

Use >, <, or =.

_____

Part B

Compare the fractions of a mile that have the same numerator.

Use >, <, or =.

_____

Part C

Use the comparisons you made.

Who lives closest to the school? _____

Who lives farthest from the school? _____

1 Jess drew point *A* on the number line.

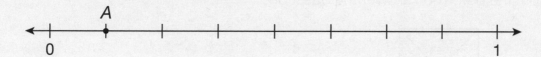

What fraction does point *A* represent? _____

What does the number line represent? What does each part of the number line represent?

```
┌────────────────────────────────────────────────┐
│                                                │
│                                                │
│                                                │
│                                                │
└────────────────────────────────────────────────┘
```

2 Which fraction represents a whole number? Mark all that apply.

○ **A.** $\frac{4}{2}$ ○ **D.** $\frac{5}{8}$

○ **B.** $\frac{5}{3}$ ○ **E.** $\frac{3}{1}$

○ **C.** $\frac{6}{6}$ ○ **F.** $\frac{4}{4}$

3 Shade each model to show a unit fraction.

 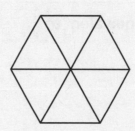

What unit fractions did you show? _____ and _____

How do you know they are unit fractions?

```
┌────────────────────────────────────────────────┐
│                                                │
│                                                │
│                                                │
└────────────────────────────────────────────────┘
```

4 Write the fraction that represents the shaded part of each model. Use numbers from the box. Then answer the question.

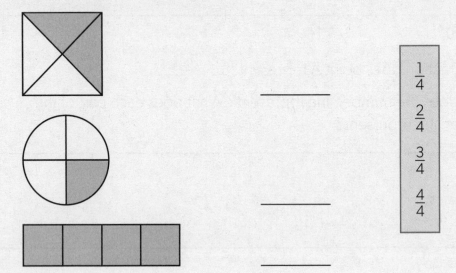

$$\frac{1}{4}$$

$$\frac{2}{4}$$

$$\frac{3}{4}$$

$$\frac{4}{4}$$

_____

_____

_____

Which fraction is a unit fraction? _____

5 Is the fraction equivalent to $\frac{1}{2}$? Write the fraction in the correct box.

| $\frac{2}{3}$ | $\frac{2}{4}$ | $\frac{3}{6}$ | $\frac{4}{6}$ | $\frac{4}{8}$ |

Equivalent to $\frac{1}{2}$	Not Equivalent to $\frac{1}{2}$

6 Ms. Frank made some costumes. The table shows the fabric she used.

Color of Fabric	Blue	Gold	Red
Amount of Fabric (in yards)	$\frac{5}{8}$	$\frac{3}{4}$	$\frac{3}{8}$

Part A

Did she use more blue fabric or red fabric? Use a number line and words to prove your answer.

Part B

Compare the amount of gold fabric to the amount of red fabric. Use >, <, or =. Explain why your answer is correct.

7 Place a point on each number line to show equivalent fractions.

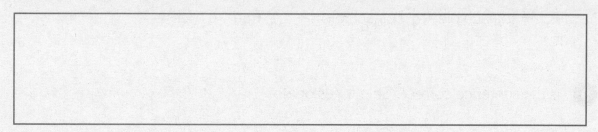

Write the equivalent fractions. _____ = _____

8 Ling made two equal-size pans of spinach pie. She cut one spinach pie into 3 equal pieces. She cut the other spinach pie into 6 equal pieces. Select True or False for each statement. Use the models to help.

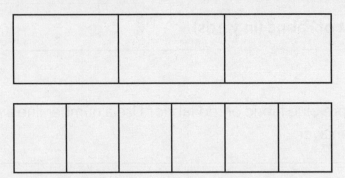

A. $\frac{1}{3}$ spinach pie $= \frac{1}{6}$ spinach pie ○ True ○ False

B. $\frac{1}{3}$ spinach pie $= \frac{2}{6}$ spinach pie ○ True ○ False

C. $\frac{2}{3}$ spinach pie $= \frac{3}{6}$ spinach pie ○ True ○ False

D. $\frac{2}{3}$ spinach pie $= \frac{4}{6}$ spinach pie ○ True ○ False

E. $\frac{3}{3}$ spinach pie $= \frac{6}{6}$ spinach pie ○ True ○ False

9 Is the sentence correct? Select Yes or No.

A. $\frac{1}{2} = \frac{1}{3}$ ○ Yes ○ No

B. $\frac{4}{6} < \frac{5}{6}$ ○ Yes ○ No

C. $\frac{5}{6} > \frac{5}{8}$ ○ Yes ○ No

D. $\frac{4}{8} < \frac{7}{8}$ ○ Yes ○ No

E. $\frac{3}{3} = \frac{3}{8}$ ○ Yes ○ No

F. $\frac{1}{4} < \frac{3}{4}$ ○ Yes ○ No

10 Eva drew the models to show equivalent fractions. She says the fractions are equivalent because both fractions are 1 part of 1 whole.

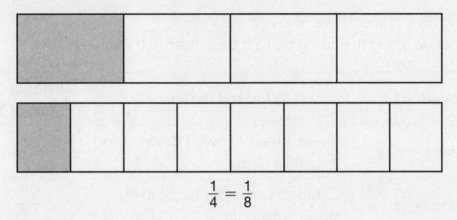

$$\frac{1}{4} = \frac{1}{8}$$

Explain the error Eva made.

Write a fraction that is equivalent to $\frac{1}{4}$ that has a denominator of 8. _____

11 Draw a line from the number line to the fraction represented on the number line.

A. •   • $\frac{5}{6}$

B. •   • $\frac{3}{3}$

C. •   • $\frac{8}{6}$

D. •   • $\frac{5}{3}$

Nature Hike

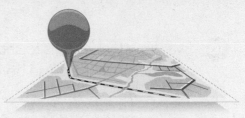

You are going on a 1-mile nature hike with your class.
Different locations along the hiking trail are described in the table below.

Location	What to Observe	Distance from Start of Trail
Tree Stumps	Beavers have chewed down trees to build a dam.	$\frac{1}{2}$ mile
Rocky Road Point	Climbers use ropes to climb the steep, rocky cliff.	$\frac{7}{8}$ mile
Wildflower Meadow	Certain types of wildflowers grow in this meadow.	$\frac{1}{4}$ mile
Deer Field	If you're quiet, you might be able to watch deer grazing in the field.	$\frac{3}{4}$ mile
Eagle's Nest	A bald eagle has built her nest at the top of a tall, bare tree.	$\frac{3}{8}$ mile

Part A Select three locations along the trail that interest you. Draw and label a number line from 0 to 1 to show the distance of each location from the start of the trail.

Part B Explain the steps you took to set up your number line and how you decided where to plot each point.

Part C What fractions could you use to show 0 and 1 on your number line? Explain your answer.

Part D Les made this number line to show the three locations he selected. Explain the errors Les made.

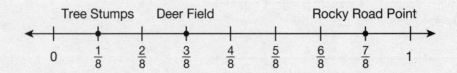

Part E Some large trees have fallen just past the $\frac{6}{8}$ mile mark. No one can get around the trees, so your class must turn around and go back to the start of the trail. Will you have seen each of the three locations you selected in Part A? Explain why or why not.

DOMAIN 4

Measurement and Data

Time

1 GETTING THE IDEA

You see and use time every day. You need to know what time it is to make sure you are not late for school or for other scheduled things that you do.

Clocks show time. Analog clocks show time using an hour hand and a minute hand. Digital clocks show the time using numbers.

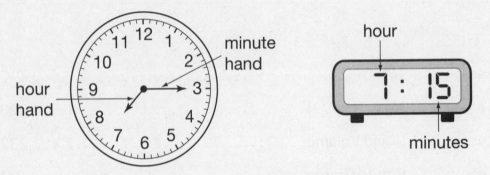

You can also measure time to determine how long an activity lasts.

Hours (hr) and **minutes (min)** are both units of time.
There are 60 minutes in 1 hour.

Example 1

What time is shown on the clock?

Strategy   Use the hour hand and minute hand to read the time.

Step 1   Find the hour.

     The hour hand is pointing between 2 and 3.

     Since the hour hand is past 2 but has not yet reached 3, the hour is 2.

Step 2   Count the minutes by 5s.

     The minute hand is pointing between 7 and 8.

     Start at 12, and count the minutes by 5s until you reach the 7.

     5, 10, 15, 20, 25, 30, 35

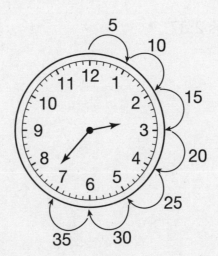

Step 3 Count the additional minutes by 1s.

Continue to count by 1s for each minute past the 7.

36, 37

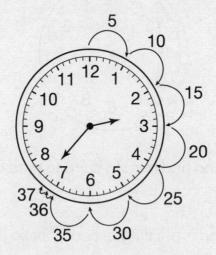

The minute hand shows 37 minutes.

Step 4 Write the time.

Time is written with a colon (:).
The hour is written before the colon, and the minutes are written after the colon.

The time is 2:37.
Read this time as "two thirty-seven."

Solution The clock shows 2:37.

Elapsed time is the amount of time that passes from the beginning to the end of an activity. For example, a class that is 2 hours long has an elapsed time of 2 hours.

Example 2

Caleb played basketball this morning. The start and end time are shown below. How long did Caleb play basketball this morning?

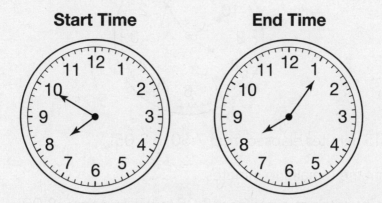

Start Time   End Time

Strategy   Count the minutes between the start time and end time.

> **Step 1**   Find the start time.
>
> The hour hand is between 7 and 8, so the hour is 7.
>
> The minute hand is on the 10. Count by 5s to 10:
> 5, 10, 15, 20, 25, 30, 35, 40, 45, 50.
>
> The minute hand shows 50 minutes.
>
> The start time is 7:50.

> **Step 2**   Find the end time.
>
> The hour hand is between 8 and 9, so the hour is 8.
>
> The minute hand shows 6 minutes.
>
> The end time is 8:06.

Step 3 Count the minutes from the start time by 5s.

Begin counting at the start time, 7:50. Count by 5s.

5, 10, 15

15 minutes elapsed from 7:50 to 8:05.

Step 4 Count the remaining minutes.

Count the minutes from 8:05 to the end time, 8:06.

Only 1 minute elapses from 8:05 to 8:06.

Step 5 Add to find the total elapsed time.

15 minutes + 1 minute = 16 minutes

Solution **Caleb played basketball for 16 minutes this morning.**

You can use a number line to help you solve word problems that involve time. Kelli's soccer practice starts at 3:30. Practice lasts 1 hour and 30 minutes. You can find the time the practice ends on the number line.

Kelli's practice ends at 5:00.

Example 3

Teana went to a movie that started at 3:30. The movie lasted for 105 minutes. What time did the movie end?

Strategy Use a number line to add units of time.

Step 1   Break apart the elapsed time into intervals.

You know that 60 minutes = 1 hour.

Write the time as a sum using 60 minutes as one of the addends.

105 minutes = 60 minutes + 45 minutes

Step 2   Draw a number line. Add the time intervals.

Draw a number line with 15-minute intervals.

Start at 3:30. Add each time interval: 60 minutes + 45 minutes.

45 minutes = 30 minutes + 15 minutes

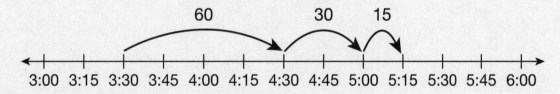

Step 3   Find the time the movie ended.

Read the number line. The end time is 5:15.

Solution The movie ended at 5:15.

Michael spent 80 minutes studying at the library. He finished studying at 4:00. What time did Michael start studying?

Break the elapsed time into intervals based on the number line.

80 minutes = 60 minutes + _____ minutes

20 minutes = _____ minutes + _____ minutes

The number line shows 10-minute intervals. Label each jump.

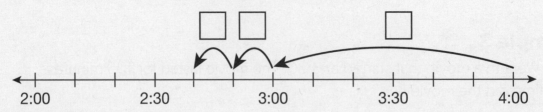

The end time is _____.

Subtract 60 minutes. The time is now _____.

Subtract 10 minutes. The time is now _____.

Subtract 10 more minutes. The time is now _____.

The start time is _____.

Michael started studying at _____.

1 Draw a line from each clock to the clock that shows the same time.

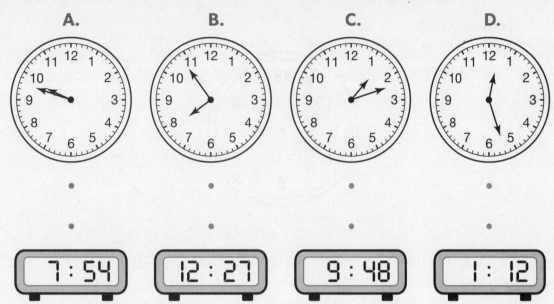

A.   **B.**   **C.**   **D.**

7:54   12:27   9:48   1:12

2 An analog clock shows the time is 8:28. Select True or False for each statement.

A. 15 minutes have elapsed since 8:13.   ○ True ○ False

B. In 12 minutes, it will be 8:40.   ○ True ○ False

C. The hour hand is between the 7 and the 8.   ○ True ○ False

D. The minute hand is between the 5 and the 6.   ○ True ○ False

3 Mia goes to soccer practice at three fifty-five.

Write the time on the digital clock.

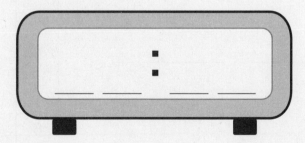

4 Draw this time on the clock.

six twenty-three

5 Look at each start time and end time. Is the elapsed time 75 minutes?
Select Yes or No.

A. Start time: 10:04   End time: 11:19   ○ Yes   ○ No

B. Start time: 5:31   End time: 6:36   ○ Yes   ○ No

C. Start time: 8:47   End time: 9:02   ○ Yes   ○ No

D. Start time: 12:52   End time: 2:07   ○ Yes   ○ No

6 It takes Juan 17 minutes to walk to school. School starts at 8:15.
What time should he leave his house to get to school on time?
Use numbers from the box to write the time.

_____ : _____ _____

| 2 |
| 3 |
| 5 |
| 7 |
| 8 |

7 Select the time shown on the clock. Mark all that apply.

- ○ **A.** eleven forty-six
- ○ **B.** twelve minutes before twelve o'clock
- ○ **C.** forty-eight minutes after eleven
- ○ **D.** twelve forty-eight
- ○ **E.** nine fifty-eight
- ○ **F.** two minutes before ten o'clock

8 Marcus worked on his homework on Saturday. He started at 20 minutes before 1:00. He worked for 30 minutes. He took a 5-minute break. Then he worked for 40 more minutes. Show the start and end times on the clocks.

Start Time

End Time

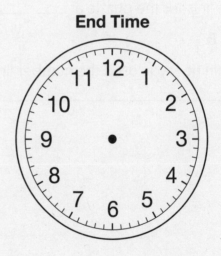

9 Danielle starts making cookies at 1:20. It takes 8 minutes to make the dough. The cookies bake for 10 minutes. Danielle lets the cookies cool for 6 minutes. Then she removes them from the pan.

What time did Danielle put the cookies in the oven? _____

What was the elapsed time from when Danielle started the dough

to when she removed the cookies from the pan? _____

10 Alicia starts a jigsaw puzzle at 4:30. It takes her 100 minutes to complete the puzzle.

Part A

What time does Alicia finish the puzzle? Show your work on a number line.

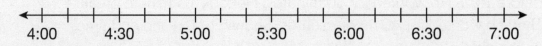

Alicia finishes the puzzle at _____.

Part B

Explain how you used the number line to find the time Alicia finished the puzzle.

LESSON 22

Mass

1 GETTING THE IDEA

Mass is the amount of matter in an object. It is similar to weight, except that mass is not affected by gravity. Mass can be measured using a scale or a balance.

Two metric units of mass are **gram (g)** and **kilogram (kg)**. Grams are used to measure the mass of smaller objects. Kilograms are used to measure the mass of larger objects.

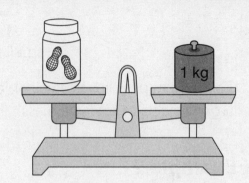

Example 1

The scale is balanced. What is the mass of the plant?

Strategy   Use a balance scale.

Step 1   Find the total mass of the weights on the right side.

There are two 1-kilogram weights.

Step 2   Find the mass of the plant.

1 kilogram + 1 kilogram = 2 kilograms

Solution   The mass of the plant is 2 kilograms.

You can **estimate** mass by using a benchmark. A **benchmark** is an object that you can use to compare other objects against. You can use these benchmarks to estimate mass.

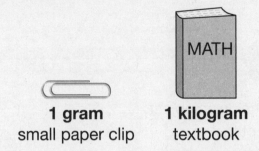

1 gram
small paper clip

1 kilogram
textbook

Compare paper clips to small objects to estimate mass. Compare a hardcover book to larger objects to estimate mass.

Example 2

Is the mass of the number cube about 5 grams or 5 kilograms?

Strategy   Use a benchmark to estimate the mass.

Step 1   Choose a benchmark.

The hardcover book is too heavy. Use the paper clip.

Step 2   Estimate the mass.

A paper clip has a mass of about 1 gram. A number cube would have a mass closer to 5 paper clips. Five textbooks would be a lot heavier than a number cube.

Solution   The number cube has a mass of about 5 grams.

Example 3

Emily measures the mass of a pumpkin and a watermelon. Together, they have a total mass of 16 kilograms. The pumpkin has a mass of 7 kilograms. What is the mass of the watermelon?

Strategy   Write and solve an equation.

Step 1   Write an equation that represents the problem.

Use w for the mass of the watermelon.

mass of pumpkin + mass of watermelon = total mass

$$7 \quad + \quad w \quad = \quad 16$$

Step 2   Solve the equation to find the mass of the watermelon.

$$7 + w = 16$$
$$7 + 9 = 16$$
$$w = 9$$

Solution   The mass of the watermelon is 9 kilograms.

Example 4

Jessica measured the mass of 5 cherries using a balance scale.

What is the mass of 1 cherry?

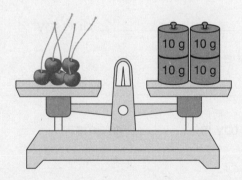

Strategy   Write and solve an equation to find the unknown mass.

Step 1	Find the mass of 5 cherries.

There are 5 cherries on the balance.
They have a total mass of 40 grams.

Step 2	Find the mass of 1 cherry.

Write an equation.

5 cherries have a mass of 40 grams.
Use multiplication or division to find the mass of 1 cherry.

Use c for the mass of 1 cherry.

$$5 \times c = 40 \qquad \text{or} \qquad 40 \div 5 = c$$

$$5 \times 8 = 40 \qquad \qquad 40 \div 5 = 8$$

Solution The mass of 1 cherry is 8 grams.

2 COACHED EXAMPLE

Jason measured the mass of two dog toys. A large toy has a mass of 45 grams. The small toy is 12 grams less than the large toy. What is the mass of the small dog toy?

The large toy has a mass of _____ grams.

The small dog toy is _____ grams less than the large toy.

You need to find the _____ of the _____ dog toy.

Write an equation to solve the problem.

Equation: _____ − _____ = _____

The mass of the small dog toy is _____ grams.

1 Which unit would you use to measure the mass of each object?
Select Gram or Kilogram.

A. spoon ○ Gram ○ Kilogram

B. suitcase ○ Gram ○ Kilogram

C. penny ○ Gram ○ Kilogram

D. lightbulb ○ Gram ○ Kilogram

E. bowling ball ○ Gram ○ Kilogram

2 Compare the mass of each object to 1 kilogram. Write the object in the correct box.

| spool of thread | backpack with books | box of toothpicks |
| bag of potatoes | a desk | pair of socks |

Less Than 1 Kilogram	Greater Than 1 Kilogram

3 Terri is mailing two packages. They have the same mass. One package has a mass of 2 kilograms. What is the total mass of both packages? Use words, numbers, or models to explain your answer.

4 Draw a line from each object to an estimate of its mass.

A. pencil •   • 5 grams

B. television •   • 200 grams

C. tiger •   • 20 kilograms

D. orange •   • 150 kilograms

5 A golf ball has a mass of 45 grams. A tennis ball has a mass of 58 grams. Select True or False for each statement.

A. The mass of the tennis ball is 13 grams less than the mass of the golf ball.   ○ True   ○ False

B. The golf ball and the tennis ball have a combined mass of 103 grams.   ○ True   ○ False

C. Two golf balls have a mass of 88 grams.   ○ True   ○ False

D. Ten tennis balls have a mass of 580 kilograms.   ○ True   ○ False

6 A nickel has a mass of 5 grams. Use the masses from the box to show the mass for each set of nickels.

3 nickels = _____ grams

10 nickels = _____ grams

20 nickels = _____ grams

| 3 |
| 10 |
| 15 |
| 25 |
| 50 |
| 100 |

7 Miranda opened a new box of cereal. She and her brother ate 64 grams of cereal. There are 276 grams of cereal left. What was the mass of the cereal before Miranda and her brother had breakfast?

Write and solve an equation for the problem.

_____

8 Sophia feeds her dog 4 kilograms of dog food per month. How much dog food does Sophia feed her dog in 6 months? Write an equation and solve.

_____

Sophia feeds her dog _____ kilograms in 6 months.

9 Manuel measured the mass of a baseball on a balance scale.

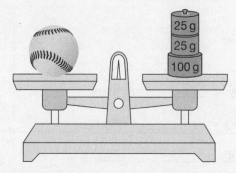

What is the mass of a baseball? _____ grams

10 Ally says her cat has a mass of about 5 grams. Is she correct? Explain your answer.

11 Lucas measured the mass of several items. His results are shown below.

- One glue stick has a mass of 10 grams.
- One glue stick and 1 crayon have a mass of 25 grams.
- One crayon and 1 pencil have a total mass of 23 grams.

Part A

What is the mass of 1 crayon? _____ grams

Show your work.

Part B

What is the mass of 1 pencil? _____ grams

Show your work.

Part C

What is the total mass of 1 crayon, 1 pencil, and 1 glue stick? _____ grams

Show your work.

Liquid Volume

1 ⬧ **GETTING THE IDEA** --

Liquid volume is the amount of liquid a container can hold. Liquid volume is also known as **capacity**. **Milliliters (mL)** and **liters (L)** are used to measure capacity. A milliliter is used to measure the capacity of smaller objects. A liter is used to measure the capacity of larger objects.

A spoon holds about 5 milliliters.

A barrel holds about 120 liters.

Example 1

How much liquid is in the container?

Strategy Read the scale.

> **Step 1** Determine the scale on the container.
>
> The marking at the top of the scale says, "mL." Each tick mark represents 1 milliliter.
>
> **Step 2** Read the measurement shown on the scale.
>
> The amount of liquid lines up with the sixth mark above the 20.
>
> It shows 26 milliliters.

Solution The container has 26 milliliters of liquid.

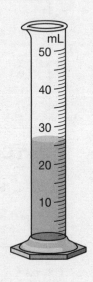

You can use benchmarks to estimate liquid volume. Remember that a **benchmark** is a known amount that can be used to **estimate** other amounts.

This dropper holds about 1 milliliter.

This water bottle holds 1 liter.

Example 2

Which of the following is the most reasonable liquid volume of the bucket?

A. 5 milliliters

B. 100 milliliters

C. 10 liters

D. 300 liters

Strategy **Use a benchmark to estimate liquid volume.**

Step 1 Choose a benchmark.

The dropper is too small. Use the water bottle.

The bucket will hold more than one bottle of water. The capacity of the bucket will be measured in liters. The answer has to be choice C or D.

Step 2 Estimate the liquid volume.

Look at the two choices. Using 10 water bottles to fill the bucket seems reasonable. The bucket could not hold 300 water bottles.

Solution A reasonable liquid volume of the bucket is 10 liters, choice C.

Example 3

A park ranger uses 24 liters of water to fill 8 birdbaths in the park. Each birdbath holds the same amount of water. What is the liquid volume of each birdbath?

Strategy   Write and solve an equation.

Step 1   Write an equation that represents the problem.

8 birdbaths have a total liquid volume of 24 liters.

Use division to find the number of liters in 1 birdbath.

$$\begin{array}{ccccc} \text{total number} & & \text{number of} & & \text{number of liters} \\ \text{of liters} & \div & \text{birdbaths} & = & \text{of 1 birdbath} \\ 24 & \div & 8 & = & \square \end{array}$$

Step 2   Solve the equation.

Use multiplication or division to find the number of liters in 1 birdbath.

$$24 \div 8 = \square \qquad \text{or} \qquad 8 \times \square = 24$$

$$24 \div 8 = 3 \qquad\qquad 8 \times 3 = 24$$

Solution   Each birdbath has a liquid volume of 3 liters.

Example 4

Ethan is using two different liquids for an experiment. He will combine both liquids into one container. What is the total liquid volume of the two liquids?

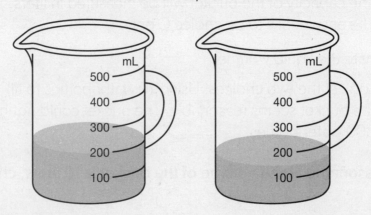

Strategy   Write and solve an equation.

Step 1   Find the liquid volume of each container.

One container has 200 milliliters of liquid.
The liquid in the other container is halfway between 100 and 200 milliliters.
Halfway between 100 and 200 is 150. So, the second container
has 150 milliliters of liquid.

Step 2   Write and solve an equation to find the total liquid volume.

$200 + 150 = \square$

$200 + 150 = 350$

Solution   The total liquid volume is 350 milliliters.

---

2 COACHED EXAMPLE

A pitcher contains 850 milliliters of lemonade. Trisha and her sister drink
440 milliliters of lemonade. How much lemonade is left in the pitcher?

To find how much is left, you need to _____.

Write an equation to solve the problem.

Equation: _____

There are _____ milliliters of lemonade left in the pitcher.

1 Which unit would you use to measure the liquid volume of each object? Select Milliliter or Liter.

A. spoon ○ Milliliter ○ Liter

B. coffee cup ○ Milliliter ○ Liter

C. fish aquarium ○ Milliliter ○ Liter

D. washing machine ○ Milliliter ○ Liter

2 How much liquid is in this container?

_____ milliliters

3 Jenny filled a watering can 4 times to water her plants. The liquid volume of her watering can is shown below. How much water did she use to water her plants?

Write an equation for the problem.

_____

Jenny used _____ liters to water all of the plants.

4 Circle the most reasonable estimate.

Juice box:
2
20
200
mL

Paint can:
4
40
400
L

5 Draw a line from each object to its estimated liquid volume.

A.  •

• 2 liters

B. •

• 15 milliliters

C.  •

• 100 liters

D. •

• 200 milliliters

6 Elijah made a large pot of soup. Is it reasonable to say he made 200 milliliters or 2 liters of soup? Explain your answer.

7 Use the metric units from the box to complete each statement.

A recycling bin has a liquid volume of 40 _____.

A paper cup has a liquid volume of 90 _____.

A bottle of perfume has a liquid volume of 120 _____.

A bathtub has a liquid volume of 150 _____.

milliliters

liters

8 Use the liquid volume shown in each container below. Select True or False for each statement.

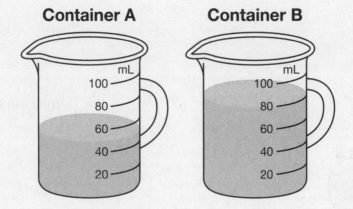

Container A   **Container B**

A. The liquid volume of Container A is 50 milliliters.   ○ True   ○ False

B. The total liquid volume of both containers is 120 milliliters.   ○ True   ○ False

C. Container B has 30 milliliters more liquid than Container A.   ○ True   ○ False

D. If 15 milliliters of liquid is poured out of Container B, it would have a volume of 60 milliliters.   ○ True   ○ False

9 Madison has a pitcher with 600 milliliters of water. She poured 150 milliliters from the pitcher into 3 test tubes. She put the same amount of water in each test tube.

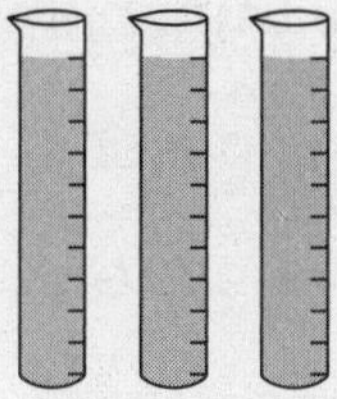

Part A

How many milliliters of water are in each test tube? _____ milliliters

Show your work.

Part B

How many milliliters of water are left in the container after she filled the test tubes? _____ milliliters

Show your work.

10 Mrs. Padilla is making punch to serve at a school meeting. She uses the recipe shown below.

> **Party Punch Recipe**
>
> 3 L fruit punch
>
> 3 L ginger ale
>
> 2 L orange juice

Part A

How many total liters of punch does the recipe make?
Show your work.

Part B

Mrs. Padilla has some pitchers to serve the punch. Each pitcher holds 2 liters. How many pitchers will Mrs. Padilla need to serve the punch she made? Explain your answer.

LESSON 24

Picture Graphs

1 GETTING THE IDEA

A **picture graph** uses symbols or pictures to show **data**. Each symbol stands for a number of things. The **key** tells you how many things each symbol stands for.

Number of Apples Picked

Ling	🍎 🍎 🍎
Grace	🍎 🍎 🍎 🍎
Jose	🍎 🍎
Kevin	🍎 🍎 🍎

Key: Each = 2 apples

The picture graph shows how many apples a group of children picked.

Each apple symbol stands for 2 picked apples.

You can multiply to find how many apples each child picked.

Multiply the number of symbols by the number each symbol stands for.

Ling: 3 × 2 = 6 apples

Grace: 4 × 2 = 8 apples

Jose: 2 × 2 = 4 apples

Kevin: 3 × 2 = 6 apples

Example 1

Some students were blowing up balloons. The table shows how many of each color balloon they blew up. Complete the picture graph.

Balloon Colors Used

Color	Number
Red	6
Blue	12
Green	8

Balloon Colors Used

Red	0 0 0
Blue	0 0 0 0 0 0
Green	

Key: Each 0 = 2 balloons

Strategy Use the key to find the number of symbols.

Step 1 Find the number of symbols needed for each color.

Each oval stands for 2 balloons.
Divide each number of balloons by 2.

Red: $6 \div 2 = 3$

Blue: $12 \div 2 = 6$

Green: $8 \div 2 = 4$

Step 2 Check the number of symbols used in the picture graph.

Red: 3 ovals ✔

Blue: 6 ovals ✔

Green: No ovals shown

Step 3 Draw ovals to finish the picture graph.

Draw 4 ovals in the row for green balloons.

Solution

Balloon Colors Used

Red	0 0 0
Blue	0 0 0 0 0 0
Green	0 0 0 0

Key: Each 0 = 2 balloons

Example 2

Students voted on their favorite soups. The table and picture graph show the results. The key is missing. How many votes does each symbol stand for?

Students' Favorite Soups

Soup	Number of Votes
Chicken Noodle	40
Chili Bean	40
Tomato	50
Vegetable	20

Students' Favorite Soups

Chicken Noodle	🥣 🥣 🥣 🥣
Chili Bean	🥣 🥣 🥣 🥣
Tomato	🥣 🥣 🥣 🥣 🥣
Vegetable	🥣 🥣

Key: Each 🥣 = _____ votes

Strategy   Divide the number of votes by the number of symbols.

Step 1   Compare the numbers and symbols.

Tomato: 50 votes, 5 bowls

$50 \div 5 = 10$

Possible Key: Each symbol stands for 10 votes.

Step 2   Check your rule. Use data in the other rows of the table.

Chicken Noodle and Chili Bean: 40 votes, 4 bowls

$40 \div 4 = 10$

Vegetable: 20 votes, 2 bowls

$20 \div 2 = 10$

The key works for each row in the table.

Solution   Each symbol stands for 10 votes.

Example 3

Students collected leaves for science class. The picture graph shows how many leaves they collected from each type of tree. Write the number of leaves of each type in the table.

Different Leaves Collected

Type of Tree	Number of Leaves
Ash	
Walnut	
Elder	
Cottonwood	
Oak	

Different Leaves Collected

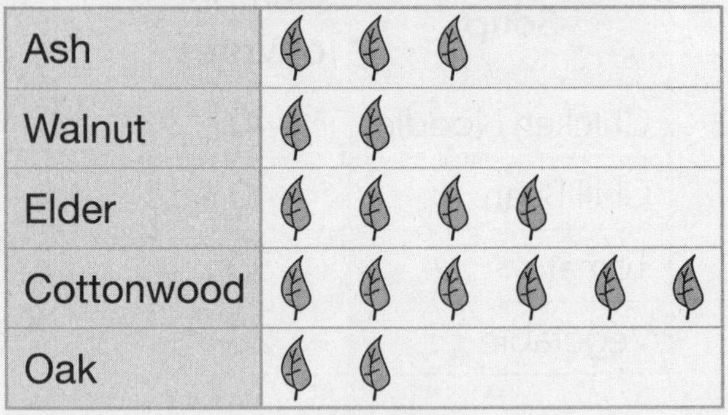

Ash	🍃 🍃 🍃
Walnut	🍃 🍃
Elder	🍃 🍃 🍃 🍃
Cottonwood	🍃 🍃 🍃 🍃 🍃 🍃
Oak	🍃 🍃

Key: Each 🍃 = 5 leaves

Strategy   Use the key.

Step 1   Count the leaf symbols in each row.

> Ash: 3 leaf symbols
>
> Walnut: 2 leaf symbols
>
> Elder: 4 leaf symbols
>
> Cottonwood: 6 leaf symbols
>
> Oak: 2 leaf symbols

Step 2   Use the key. Multiply the number of leaf symbols by 5.

> Ash: 3 × 5 = 15
>
> Walnut: 2 × 5 = 10
>
> Elder: 4 × 5 = 20
>
> Cottonwood: 6 × 5 = 30
>
> Oak: 2 × 5 = 10

Step 3 Write the number of each type of leaf in the table.

Different Leaves Collected

Type of Tree	Number of Leaves
Ash	**15**
Walnut	**10**
Elder	**20**
Cottonwood	**30**
Oak	**10**

Solution The table in Step 3 shows the number of leaves collected.

② COACHED EXAMPLE --

Students named their favorite yogurt flavors. The table shows the students' votes. Complete the picture graph.

Favorite Fruit Yogurt Flavors

Yogurt	Number of Votes
Strawberry	20
Blueberry	15
Peach	10

Favorite Fruit Yogurt Flavors

Strawberry	♡ ♡ ♡ ♡
Blueberry	
Peach	♡ ♡

Key: Each ♡ = _____ votes

How many votes does each heart stand for?

Divide the number of _____ in the table by the number of _____.

Strawberry: 20 ÷ _____ = _____   Peach : 10 ÷ _____ = _____

Each heart stands for _____ votes.

Find the number of hearts needed to show the blueberry votes.

_____ ÷ _____ = _____

Complete the graph.

Each heart stands for _____ votes. Draw _____ hearts for blueberry.

1 Students read books during vacation. The picture graph shows how many books they read.

Number of Books Read

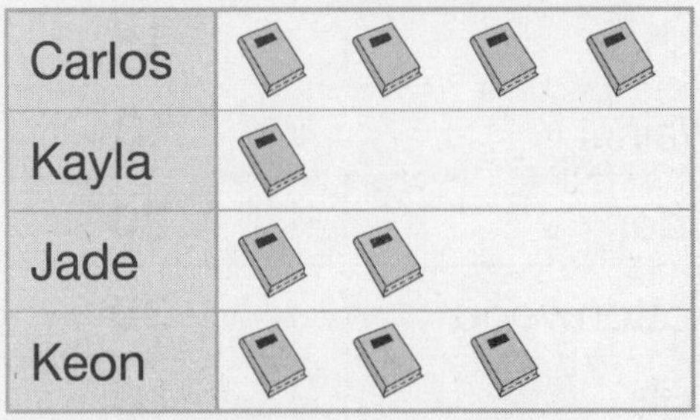

Carlos	📖 📖 📖 📖
Kayla	📖
Jade	📖 📖
Keon	📖 📖 📖

Key: Each 📖 = 2 books

Is the statement about the graph correct? Select True or False.

A. Carlos read the most books. ○ True ○ False

B. Carlos read 4 books. ○ True ○ False

C. Carlos read 8 books. ○ True ○ False

D. Jade read 2 more books than Kayla read. ○ True ○ False

E. Together, the students read a total of 10 books. ○ True ○ False

2 Natalie and Jose counted the frogs they saw on a camping trip. Natalie saw 12 frogs. Jose saw 20 frogs. Use the key to complete the picture graph.

Number of Frogs Counted

Natalie	
Jose	

Key: Each ● = 2 frogs

3 The picture graph shows the number of tacos sold.

Number of Tacos Sold

Monday	🌮 🌮 🌮 🌮 🌮
Wednesday	🌮 🌮 🌮 🌮 🌮 🌮
Friday	🌮 🌮 🌮 🌮 🌮 🌮 🌮 🌮 🌮

Key: Each  🌮 = 10 tacos

Use numbers from the box to complete the table.

Lunch Day	Number Sold
Monday	
Wednesday	
Friday	

5	18
6	50
9	60
10	90

4 An art teacher asked her students to choose a shape to make a design. The table shows the number of students who chose each shape.

Shape	Number of Students
Triangle	6
Square	16
Rectangle	10

Kylie wants to make a picture graph. Each ✓ will stand for 2 students. How many check marks should she use for each shape?

Triangle: _____   Square: _____   Rectangle: _____

5 The table and graph show the number of shells collected by 3 children. Complete the key to find the number that each symbol stands for.

Shells Collected

Name	Number of Shells
Duane	20
Sarah	8
Emma	16

Shells Collected

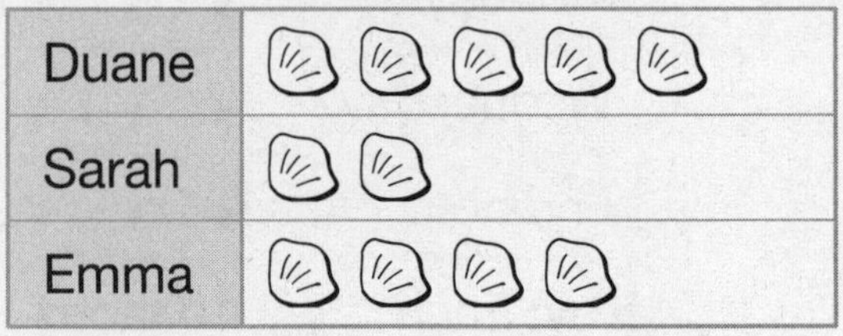

Duane	🐚 🐚 🐚 🐚 🐚
Sarah	🐚 🐚
Emma	🐚 🐚 🐚 🐚

Key: Each 🐚 = _____ shells

6 The picture graph shows the number of different kinds of toys in a store.

Toys on Store Shelves

Board games	✦ ✦ ✦ ✦ ✦ ✦ ✦ ✦ ✦
Dolls	✦ ✦ ✦ ✦
Stuffed animals	✦ ✦ ✦ ✦ ✦ ✦ ✦ ✦ ✦ ✦
Puzzles	✦ ✦ ✦ ✦ ✦
Models	✦ ✦

Key: Each ✦ = 5 toys

Is the statement about the picture graph correct? Select True or False.

A. There are 40 dolls.　　　　　　　　　○ True　○ False

B. There are 45 board games.　　　　　○ True　○ False

C. There are fewer models than dolls.　○ True　○ False

D. There are 25 puzzles.　　　　　　　○ True　○ False

E. There are 3 more puzzles than there are models.　　　　　　　○ True　○ False

7 Parents at Center School were asked if they liked summer or winter vacations best. Mario wants to make a picture graph.

Season	Number of Votes
Summer	20
Winter	40

Part A

Mario will draw one sun for every 5 votes. How many suns should he draw for summer? Show your work.

_____

Part B

Mario changed his mind. He will draw one sun for every 10 votes. How many suns should he draw for winter? Show your work.

_____

Part C

Is there another key that is reasonable to use with this data? Explain.

Bar Graphs

A **bar graph** uses horizontal or vertical bars to show **data**. The **scale** is a set of equally spaced numbers used as labels on a graph.

To read a picture graph, you use the key and the number of symbols to determine each amount.

Students' Favorite Fruits

Apple	☺ ☺ ☺ ☺
Peach	☺
Banana	☺ ☺ ☺

Key: Each ☺ = 5 votes

To read a bar graph, you match the height or length of the bar with the numbers on the scale. Here are horizontal and vertical bar graphs for the same data as the picture graph.

Vertical bar graph

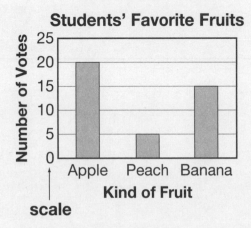

Horizontal bar graph

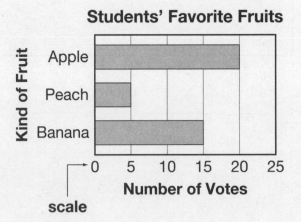

Example 1

Third grade students named their favorite kinds of juice. The table shows the data. Complete the bar graph.

Favorite Juice

Juice	Number of Votes
Grape	16
Apple	10
Cranberry	8
Orange	14

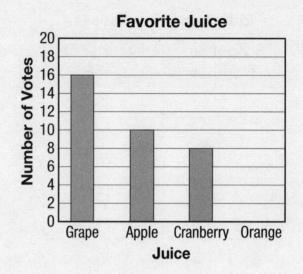

Strategy   Use the data and the scale to find the height of the bar.

Step 1   Find the scale on the bar graph.

The numbers on the left side of the bar graph show the scale. It shows counting by 2s.

Step 2   Find the number of votes for orange juice in the table.

The table shows 14 students voted for orange juice.

Step 3   Draw a bar to represent the data for orange juice.

Start at 0. The bar for orange juice should end at the line for 14 on the scale.

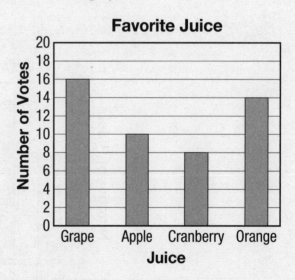

Solution   The completed graph is shown in Step 3.

Example 2

The table shows the number of students who ride different school buses to Circle Elementary. Complete the bar graph.

Riders on School Buses

School Bus Number	Number of Riders
Bus 1	30
Bus 2	45
Bus 3	50
Bus 4	25
Bus 5	35

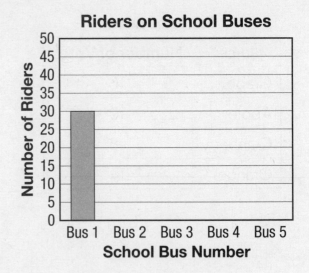

Strategy   Use the data and the scale to find the height of each bar.

Step 1   Look at the scale on the bar graph.

The scale shows counting by 5s.

Step 2   Find the number of riders for each bus in the table.

30 riders for Bus 1, 45 riders for Bus 2, 50 riders for Bus 3, 25 riders for Bus 4, and 35 riders for Bus 5

Step 3   Draw a bar to represent the data for each bus.

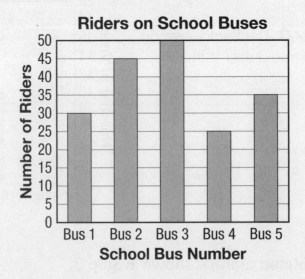

Solution   The completed graph is shown in Step 3.

Example 3

Valley Elementary began fund-raising for a new playground. The graph shows the amount of money raised in the first few days. How much more money was collected on Thursday than on Monday?

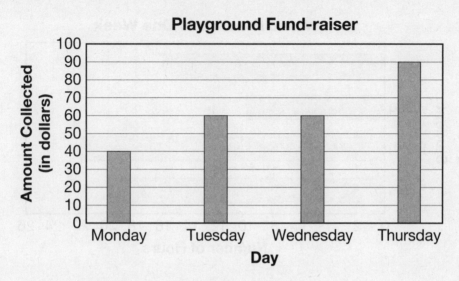

Playground Fund-raiser

Strategy	Compare the heights of the bars.

Step 1 Find how much was collected on Thursday and Monday.

Monday: $40 collected

Thursday: $90 collected

Step 2 Decide which operation to use.

To find *how much more*, you must subtract. Subtract the amount collected on Monday from the amount collected on Thursday.

90 − 40 = 50

Solution $50 more was collected on Thursday than on Monday.

Example 4

Four music students recorded the total number of hours they practiced their instruments each week. Which pair of students together practiced longer, Anna and Luis or Ling and Farah?

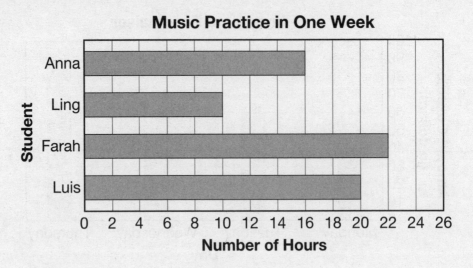

Music Practice in One Week

Strategy	Use the lengths of the bars to find the amount of hours practiced, then compare.

Step 1	Find the amount of hours practiced by Anna and Luis, then find the sum of those numbers.

Anna: 16 hours   Luis: 20 hours

16 + 20 = 36 hours

Step 2	Find the amount of hours practiced by Ling and Farah, then find the sum of those numbers.

Ling: 10 hours   Farah: 22 hours

10 + 22 = 32 hours

Step 3	Compare the hours practiced by the pairs of students.

36 > 32

Solution	Anna and Luis practiced more hours than Ling and Farah.

The graph shows the lengths of some bicycle trails in a city. Steve rides two trails for a total of 40 miles. Which two trails did he ride?

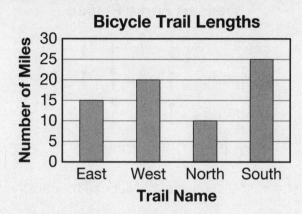

Add each pair of trails to find the _____.

Write Yes or No depending on whether the sum is 40 miles.

East and West: 15 + _____ = _____   No, the sum is _____ miles.

East and North: 15 + _____ = _____   No, the sum is _____ miles.

East and South: _____ + 25 = _____   _____, the sum is _____ miles.

West and North: _____ + _____ = _____   _____, the sum is _____ miles.

West and South: _____ + _____ = _____   _____, the sum is _____ miles.

North and South: _____ + _____ = _____   _____, the sum is _____ miles.

Steve rides the _____ and _____ trails.

1 The picture graph shows the number of forks three children put on tables for a party.

Dessert Forks Placed

Ava	🍴 🍴 🍴 🍴
Brianna	🍴 🍴 🍴 🍴 🍴
Ethan	🍴 🍴 🍴

Key: Each 🍴 = 2 forks

Which bar graph shows the same data? Mark all that apply.

○ A.

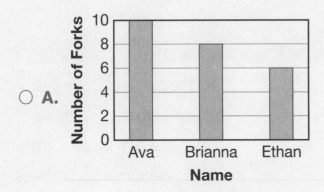

○ B.

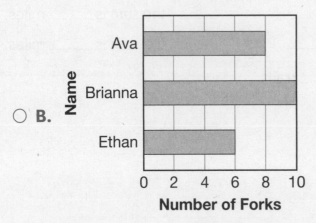

○ C.

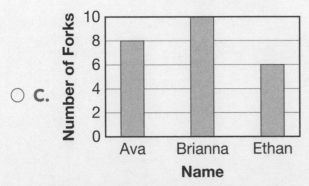

2 The graph shows the number of cars in the parking lot each weekday.

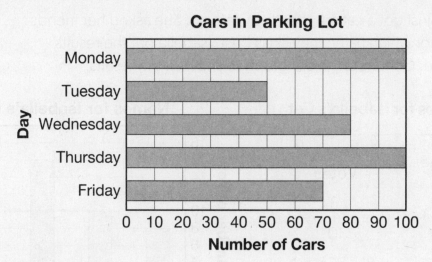

Cars in Parking Lot

Which statement about the data is true? Mark all that apply.

○ **A.** The fewest number of cars were parked on Tuesday.

○ **B.** There were more cars in the lot on Friday than on Wednesday.

○ **C.** The same number of cars were parked on Monday and Thursday.

○ **D.** There were 400 cars parked in the lot in that week in all.

○ **E.** There were 70 cars parked on Wednesday.

3 A teacher asked his students which pet they prefer: cat, dog, or bird. The students' responses are shown below.

dog cat cat dog dog dog bird cat cat cat dog dog cat dog bird dog

Count the votes for each pet. Fill in the table, and complete the bar graph.

Favorite Pets

Pet	Number of Votes
Bird	
Cat	
Dog	

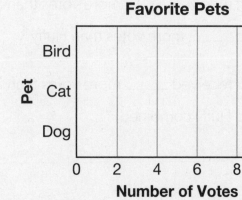

Favorite Pets

Use the table below for problems 4 and 5.

4 Isabella just got a cat and needs to name it. She asked her friends to vote for which name they liked best. Isabella put the results in a table. Complete the bar graph to show all the results.

Names for Isabella's Cat

Name	Number of Votes
Fluffy	8
Ginger	10
Puff	16
Shadow	4

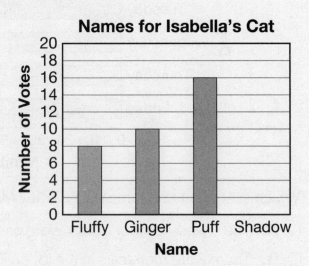

Names for Isabella's Cat

5 Write a number or a word from the box to make each statement true.

Puff received _____ votes. It received the

_____ number of votes of all

the names.

Puff received _____ more votes than Shadow

and _____ more votes than Fluffy.

Puff received _____ more votes than Shadow

and Fluffy combined.

| fewest |
| most |
| 4 |
| 8 |
| 10 |
| 12 |
| 16 |

6 A bakery recorded the number of muffins sold in the morning. The bar graph below shows the results.

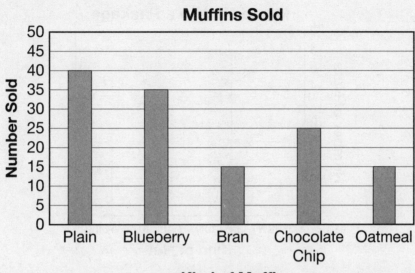

Select True or False for each statement about the muffin sales.

A. More plain muffins were sold than any other kind.

○ True ○ False

B. Twenty-five chocolate chip muffins were sold.

○ True ○ False

C. More bran muffins than oatmeal muffins were sold.

○ True ○ False

D. Twenty more bran muffins than blueberry muffins were sold.

○ True ○ False

E. Ten fewer chocolate chip muffins than blueberry muffins were sold.

○ True ○ False

7 Matt and Emma counted the number of different kinds of nuts in a package of mixed nuts. The bar graph below shows their data.

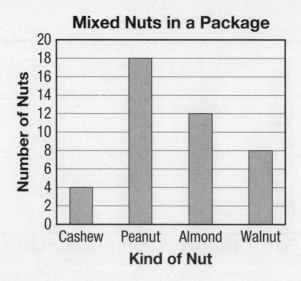

Part A

How many nuts were in the package in all? Show your work.

Part B

How many more peanuts and almonds were in the package than cashews and walnuts? Explain how you found your answer.

LESSON 26

Line Plots

1 GETTING THE IDEA

A **line plot** is a way of showing data on a number line. **Data** is information collected about people or things.

A librarian measured the widths of some books on a shelf. The table below shows the results.

Width of Books

Width (in inches)	Number of Books
$\frac{1}{4}$	4
$\frac{2}{4}$	2
$\frac{3}{4}$	1

The line plot shows the data from the table. Each X stands for 1 book.

Width of Books

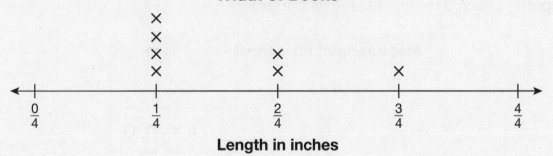

Length in inches

Example 1

Find the measurement of each line. Measure to the nearest $\frac{1}{2}$ inch. Record the measurements in a table.

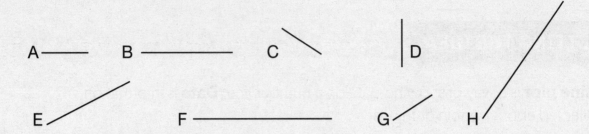

Strategy   **Use a ruler. Record the measurements.**

Step 1   Use an inch ruler to measure each line.

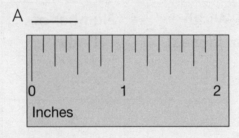

Step 2   Record your measurements.

Line A: $\frac{1}{2}$ inch   Line B: 1 inch   Line C: $\frac{1}{2}$ inch   Line D: $\frac{1}{2}$ inch

Line E: 1 inch   Line F: $1\frac{1}{2}$ inches   Line G: $\frac{1}{2}$ inch   Line H: $1\frac{1}{2}$ inches

Step 3   Record the measurements in a table.

Measurement (in inches)	Line
0	
$\frac{1}{2}$	A, C, D, G
1	B, E
$1\frac{1}{2}$	F, H
2	

Solution   The table is shown in Step 3.

Example 2

Draw a line plot for the measurements in Example 1.

Strategy **Make one X on the line plot for each measurement.**

Step 1 Draw and label a number line with $\frac{1}{2}$ inch intervals.

Mark equal spaces on a number line.

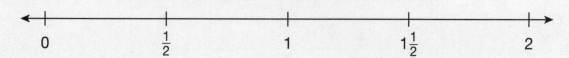

Step 2 Mark an X for each measurement.

Four lines measured $\frac{1}{2}$ inch, so make four Xs above the mark for $\frac{1}{2}$.

Two lines measured 1 inch, so make two Xs above the mark for 1.

Two lines measured $1\frac{1}{2}$ inches, so make two Xs above the mark for $1\frac{1}{2}$.

Label the title and the number line.

Line Measurements

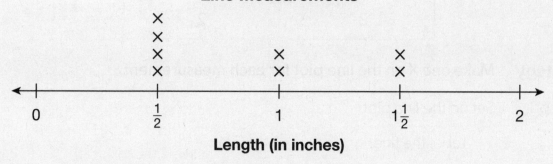

Length (in inches)

Solution The line plot is shown in Step 2.

Example 3

Students printed their first and last names. Then they measured the length of their printed names to the nearest $\frac{1}{4}$ inch. They put the measurements in a table. Display the data on a line plot.

Name Lengths

Length (in inches)	Number of Names
$1\frac{2}{4}$	1
$1\frac{3}{4}$	0
2	5
$2\frac{1}{4}$	6
$2\frac{2}{4}$	3
$2\frac{3}{4}$	4
3	2

Strategy   Make one X on the line plot for each measurement.

Step 1   Set up the line plot.

Label the title.

Label the number line.

The data go from $1\frac{2}{4}$ to 3 inches by $\frac{1}{4}$ inch.

Mark the number line in fourths.

Name Lengths

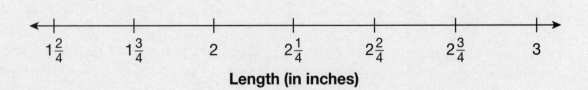

Length (in inches)

Step 2   Mark an X for each measurement.

Place the Xs above the correct number on the line.

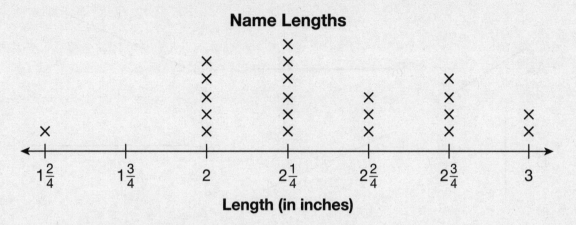

Name Lengths

Length (in inches)

Solution   The line plot of the data is shown in Step 2.

Measure each line to the nearest $\frac{1}{4}$ inch. Display the data on a line plot.

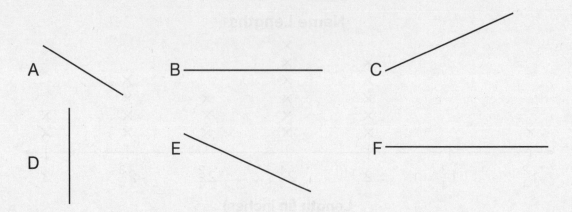

Use an inch ruler to measure the length of each line.

Line A: _____ inch(es)   Line B: _____ inch(es)   Line C: _____ inch(es)

Line D: _____ inch(es)   Line E: _____ inch(es)   Line F: _____ inch(es)

Record the measurements in the table.

Line Measurements

Length (in inches)	Line
1	
$1\frac{1}{4}$	
$1\frac{2}{4}$	
$1\frac{3}{4}$	
2	

Make the line plot.

The title is labeled.

The number line is labeled in fourths from 1 to 2.

Draw the Xs.

Draw _____ X(s) above 1.

Draw _____ X(s) above $1\frac{1}{4}$.

Draw _____ X(s) above $1\frac{2}{4}$.

Draw _____ X(s) above $1\frac{3}{4}$.

Draw _____ X(s) above 2.

Line Measurements

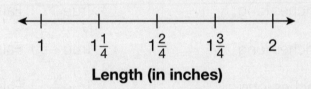

Length (in inches)

1 Alex and Biance measured the lines with a ruler. Alex measured Line A. Bianca measured line B.

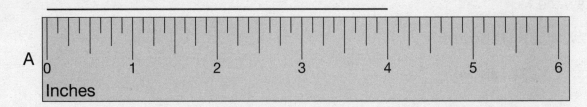

A

Inches

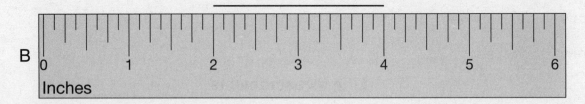

B

Inches

Look at the measurements. Select True or False for each statement.

A. Line A is 2 inches long. ○ True ○ False

B. Line A is 4 inches long. ○ True ○ False

C. Line B is 4 inches long. ○ True ○ False

D. Lines A and B are the same length. ○ True ○ False

2 Draw a line plot for these data.

2	2	$\frac{1}{2}$	1	$2\frac{1}{2}$
$2\frac{1}{2}$	2	$2\frac{1}{2}$	1	$1\frac{1}{2}$
$1\frac{1}{2}$	$1\frac{1}{2}$	$\frac{1}{2}$	$1\frac{1}{2}$	2
2	2	$2\frac{1}{2}$	$\frac{1}{2}$	$2\frac{1}{2}$

3 Students looked at a block and guessed its length. Their guesses are recorded in the table.

Length (in inches)	Number of Students
3	5
$3\frac{1}{2}$	8
4	6
$4\frac{1}{2}$	0
5	1
$5\frac{1}{2}$	1

Use the numbers in the box to complete the statements.

In a line plot of the data:

The tallest column of Xs will be above _____.

There will be 5 Xs above _____.

There will be 1 X above _____ and _____.

$$3$$
$$3\frac{1}{2}$$
$$4$$
$$4\frac{1}{2}$$
$$5$$
$$5\frac{1}{2}$$

The numbers below are the lengths, in inches, of some magnets. Use the data for problems 4–6.

| $3\frac{1}{4}$ | $2\frac{1}{4}$ | $2\frac{1}{4}$ | $2\frac{2}{4}$ | $3\frac{1}{4}$ | $3\frac{1}{4}$ | $2\frac{2}{4}$ | 3 | $3\frac{1}{4}$ | $2\frac{2}{4}$ |

4 Record the number of magnets of each length in the table.

Magnet Measurements

Length (in inches)	Number of Magnets
$2\frac{1}{4}$	
$2\frac{2}{4}$	
$2\frac{3}{4}$	
3	
$3\frac{1}{4}$	

5 Select True or False for each statement about how to make a line plot from the data in the table.

A. The line plot will have Xs above every measurement in the table.   ○ True   ○ False

B. The number line should be marked in fourths.   ○ True   ○ False

C. The number line should be marked from $2\frac{1}{4}$ to $3\frac{1}{4}$.   ○ True   ○ False

D. There will be 3 Xs above $2\frac{2}{4}$.   ○ True   ○ False

E. The most Xs will be above $2\frac{2}{4}$.   ○ True   ○ False

6 Display the data from the table on a line plot.

Magnet Measurements

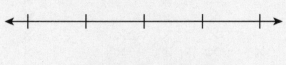

Length (in inches)

7 The line plot shows data about the lengths of small objects in a classroom.

Classroom Object Measurements

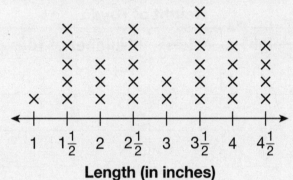

Length (in inches)

Is the statement about the line plot true? Select Yes or No.

A. There were 3 objects that measured 3 inches.　　　　　　　　　○ Yes　○ No

B. There were 8 objects that measured either 2 or $2\frac{1}{2}$ inches.　　　　　　○ Yes　○ No

C. There were 5 objects that measured from 1 to $1\frac{1}{2}$ inches.　　　　　　　○ Yes　○ No

D. The same number of objects measured $1\frac{1}{2}$ inches and $2\frac{1}{2}$ inches.　　　○ Yes　○ No

E. Each X stands for one measurement, so there were 30 measurements.　　○ Yes　○ No

8 The line plot shows the number of students who have toys of different heights.

Height of Toys

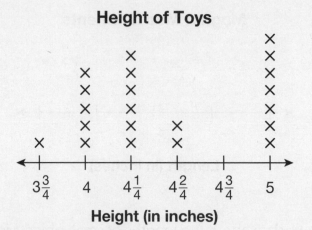

Height (in inches)

Use the line plot to fill in the data table.

Height of Toys

Height (in inches)	Number of Toys
$3\frac{3}{4}$	
4	
$4\frac{1}{4}$	
$4\frac{2}{4}$	
$4\frac{3}{4}$	
5	

LESSON 27

Perimeter

Perimeter is the distance around a figure. It is the sum of the lengths of the sides of the figure.

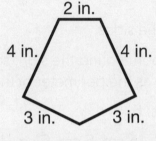

$$2 + 4 + 3 + 3 + 4 = 16$$

The perimeter of the figure is 16 inches.

You can use perimeter in many ways. For example, to put a fence around a garden, you need to find the perimeter of the garden. Then you know the length of fence you need.

Also, you may want to put yarn around a photo. When you find the perimeter of the photo, you know the length of yarn you need.

Example 1

Ellie put ribbon around the sign below. What is the length of the ribbon?

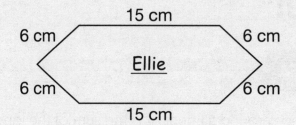

Strategy **Find the sum of the lengths of the sides.**

Step 1 Find the lengths of the sides.

Ellie put the ribbon around the sign, so the ribbon is the same length as the perimeter of the sign.

Number of sides: 6

Lengths of sides: 15 cm, 6 cm, 6 cm, 15 cm, 6 cm, 6 cm

Step 2 Find the sum of the lengths of the sides.

$$15 + 6 + 6 + 15 + 6 + 6 =$$

You can group the lengths to make the addition easier.

$$(15 + 15) + (6 + 6 + 6 + 6) = 30 + 24$$
$$= 54$$

The perimeter of the sign is 54 centimeters.

Solution **The length of the ribbon is 54 centimeters.**

For regular figures, where all the sides of the figure are the same length, you can multiply to find the perimeter. Multiply the length of one side by the number of sides in the figure.

Example 2

Find the perimeter of the pentagon.

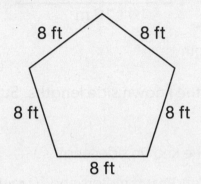

Strategy   Find the sum of the lengths of the sides. Check your work by multiplying.

Step 1   Make a list of what you know.

   Number of sides: 5

   Length of each side: 8 feet

Step 2   Find the sum of the lengths of the sides.

   $8 + 8 + 8 + 8 + 8 = 40$

   The perimeter is 40 feet.

Step 3   Check by multiplying.

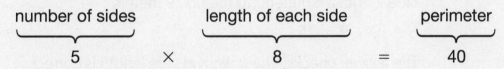

number of sides	length of each side	perimeter
5	× 8	= 40

   The perimeter is 40 feet.

Solution   The perimeter of the pentagon is 40 feet.

Example 3

The perimeter of the triangle is 25 meters.

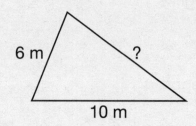

What is the unknown side length?

Strategy **Find the sum of the known side lengths. Subtract the sum from the perimeter.**

Step 1   Find the sum of the known side lengths.

Known side lengths: 6 meters and 10 meters

$6 + 10 = 16$

Step 2   Subtract the sum from the perimeter.

Perimeter: 25 meters

Sum of the known side lengths: 16 meters

$25 - 16 = 9$

The unknown side length is 9 meters.

Step 3   Check your answer.

Find the perimeter of the figure.
The perimeter should be 25 meters.

Side lengths: 6 meters, 10 meters, 9 meters

$6 + 10 + 9 = 25$

The answer checks. The unknown side length is correct.

Solution   **The unknown side length is 9 meters.**

This figure has a perimeter of 58 inches.

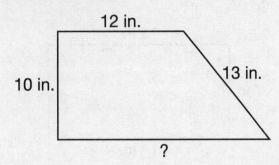

What is the unknown side length?

First, find the _____ of the known side lengths.

_____ + _____ + _____ = _____

Next, subtract the _____ of the known side lengths from the _____.

_____ − _____ = _____

Finally, put the unknown side length in the equation to check your answer.

_____ + _____ + _____ + _____ = _____.

The unknown side length of the figure is _____ inches.

1 Eli bought the tray below.

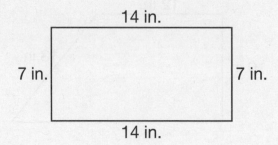

14 in.

7 in.   7 in.

14 in.

Select True or False for each statement.

A. The tray has a perimeter of 42 inches.   ○ True   ○ False

B. The tray has a perimeter of 35 inches.   ○ True   ○ False

C. You can multiply 14 × 4 to find the perimeter.   ○ True   ○ False

D. You can multiply 7 × 4 to find the perimeter.   ○ True   ○ False

2 What is the perimeter of the figure?

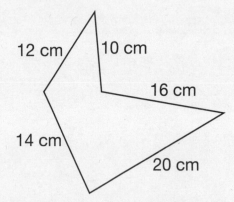

12 cm   10 cm

16 cm

14 cm

20 cm

Equation: _____

The perimeter of the figure is _____ centimeters.

3 Draw a line from each figure to its perimeter.

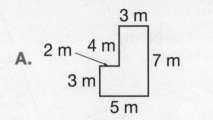

A. •

• 21 meters

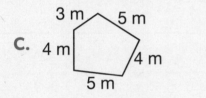

B. •

• 22 meters

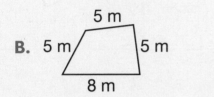

C. •

• 23 meters

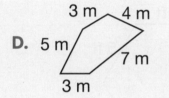

D. •

• 24 meters

4 Jill made this banner for her room. The perimeter of the banner is 43 inches. What is the length of the unknown side?

Circle the number that makes the statement true.

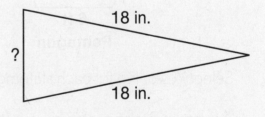

The unknown side length of the banner is

| 6 in. |
| 7 in. |
| 8 in. |

.

5 Paola rode her bike one time around the park shown.

How many meters did Paola ride her bike?

_____ meters

How did you find your answer? Explain.

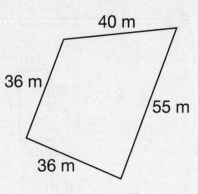

---

6 Jorge drew these two figures.

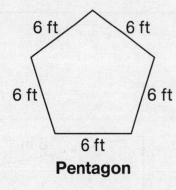

Pentagon

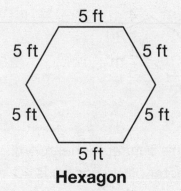

Hexagon

Select Yes or No for each statement.

A. perimeter of pentagon > perimeter of hexagon   ○ Yes ○ No

B. perimeter of pentagon = perimeter of hexagon   ○ Yes ○ No

C. perimeter of hexagon = 5 + 5 + 5 + 5 + 5 + 5   ○ Yes ○ No

D. perimeter of pentagon = 6 × 6   ○ Yes ○ No

7 A farmer put a fence around a pasture. Below is a drawing of the pasture.

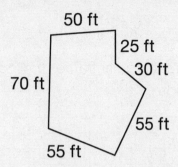

How many feet of fence did the farmer use? Complete the equation.
Solve the problem.

_____ + _____ + _____ + _____ + _____ = _____

The farmer used _____ feet of fence.

8 Ms. Baez asked her students to find the side lengths of this rectangle.
The perimeter of the rectangle is 40 feet.

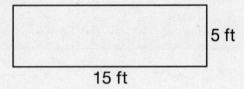

Al says he needs more information to find the side lengths.
Mia says there is enough information. Who is correct?

_____

Explain your answer.

_____

9 Sal made a frame that is in the shape of a rectangle. He used exactly 20 inches of wood.

Part A

Use the grid to draw two rectangular frames that Sal might have made. Label the sides of each photo.

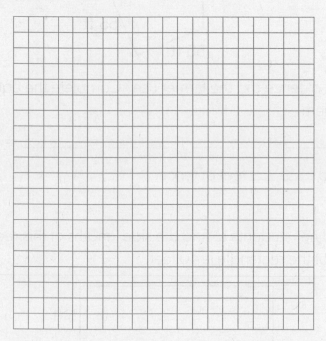

Part B

Explain why each frame would fit each of the photos.

3.MD.5.a, 3.MD.5.b, 3.MD.6, 3.MD.7.a

Understanding Area

Area is the measure of the amount of space that covers a figure. It is measured in square units. Look at the square on the right. Each side length is 1 unit. A square with side lengths of 1 unit is called a **unit square**.

You can use the unit square to measure area.

Remember that area is different from perimeter. Area is the measure of what covers a figure. Perimeter is the distance around a figure.

Example 1

Find the area of the unit square.

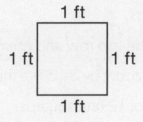

Strategy	Use the meaning of unit square.
Step 1	Check that each side length is 1 unit.
	Each side length of the unit square is 1 foot.
	The square is a unit square.
Step 2	Find the area of the unit square.
	Read the unit on the square.
	The unit is feet.
	The area is 1 square foot.
Solution	The area of the unit square is 1 square foot.

You can cover a plane figure in unit squares. The number of unit squares that cover the figure is its area. There can be no gaps or overlaps in the unit squares.

Example 2

Find the area of the rectangle.

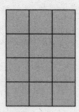

▨ = 1 square unit

Strategy	Count the unit squares.

Step 1 Read the unit on the unit square.

Each unit square is 1 square unit.

The area of the rectangle will be in square units.

Step 2 Count the unit squares.

You can start at the top row and count by 1s.

You can also skip count by 3s, since there are 3 unit squares in each row.

There are a total of 12 unit squares.

Step 3 Find the area.

There are 12 unit squares in the rectangle.

Each unit square is 1 square unit.

12 unit squares = 12 square units

Solution The area of the rectangle is 12 square units.

Example 3

Find the area of the figure.

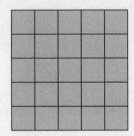

□ = 1 square centimeter

Strategy   Count the unit squares.

Step 1   Read the unit on the unit square.

Each unit square is 1 square centimeter.

The area of the rectangle will be in square centimeters.

Step 2   Count the unit squares.

You can start at the top row and count by 1s.

There are 5 unit squares in each row. You can also skip count by 5s.

There are a total of 25 unit squares.

Step 3   Check your answer.

If you can skip count by 5s, that means you can multiply by 5.

There are 5 unit squares in each row. There are 5 rows.

$5 \times 5 = 25$

There are a total of 25 unit squares.

Step 4   Find the area.

There are 25 unit squares in the rectangle.

Each unit square is 1 square centimeter.

25 unit squares = 25 square centimeters

Solution   **The area of the rectangle is 25 square centimeters.**

Find the area of the rectangle.

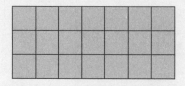

= 1 square inch

You need to know the unit with which you will be measuring the area.

Each unit square is 1 square _____.

Next, count the number of _____ _____.

There are a total of _____ unit squares.

After you have added or counted, you can _____ to check the answer.

There are _____ unit squares in each row. There are _____ rows.

_____ × _____ = _____

Finally, find the _____.

_____ unit squares = _____ square inches

The area of the rectangle is _____ square inches.

1 Leonie used the unit square below to measure the area of a rectangle.

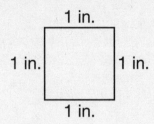

Select Yes or No for each statement.

A. The unit square is 1 square inch.　　　○ Yes　○ No

B. The unit square is 4 square inches.　　　○ Yes　○ No

C. All unit squares are the same size.　　　○ Yes　○ No

D. Leonie used the unit square to　　　　　○ Yes　○ No
measure perimeter.

2 Justine found the area of the rectangle. She used multiplication to check her answer.

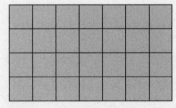

■ = 1 square meter

Use the numbers in the box. Find the area of the rectangle. Show how to use multiplication to check the answer.

4	20
5	24
6	28
7	30

The area is _____ square meters.

_____ × _____ = _____

3 Draw a line from each figure to its area. The unit square in each figure is 1 square centimeter.

A. 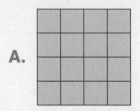 • • 12 square centimeters

B. 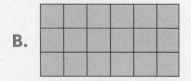 • • 15 square centimeters

C. 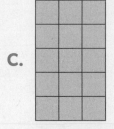 • • 16 square centimeters

D. 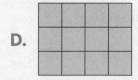 • • 18 square centimeters

4 Mr. James laid out a new lawn made of patches of grass. Each patch of grass is 1 square foot.

What is the area of the lawn?

_____ square feet

Explain how you found your answer.

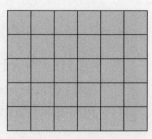

5 Nina made a picture with square tiles.

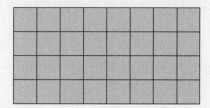

⬜ = 1 square centimeter

Select True or False for each statement.

A. The area of the picture is 24 square centimeters.   ○ True   ○ False

B. The area of the picture is 32 square centimeters.   ○ True   ○ False

C. Add 8 + 8 + 4 + 4 to find the number of tiles Nina used.   ○ True   ○ False

D. Multiply 4 × 8 to find the number of tiles Nina used.   ○ True   ○ False

6 Find the area of each figure. Write the letter of each figure in the correct box. Each unit square in a figure is 1 square meter.

A

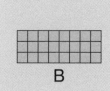

B

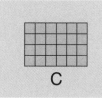

C

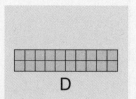

D

20 Square Meters	24 Square Meters

7 Raj covered a card in stamps. Each stamp is 1 square inch. There are 6 rows of stamps. There are 6 stamps in each row.

Part A

Use the grid. Draw the card that Raj covered in stamps.

Part B

What is the area of the card?

_____ square inches

Part C

Describe two ways you can find the area of the card.

8 Compare the areas of the rectangles. Each unit square is 1 square unit.

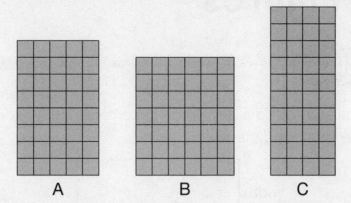

A   B   C

Is the comparison true? Mark all that apply.

○ **A.** Area of A = Area of C   ○ **D.** Area of A = Area of B

○ **B.** Area of B > Area of C   ○ **E.** Area of C < Area of B

○ **C.** Area of B < Area of A   ○ **F.** Area of C > Area of A

9 The area of the figure is 45 square units. Each unit square is 1 square unit.

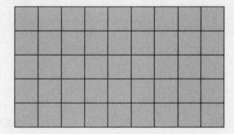

How does the area change if you add one row of unit squares? Use words and numbers to explain your answer.

Area of Figures

1 ▶ GETTING THE IDEA

A **rectangle** is a figure with 4 sides and 4 square corners. The sides are referred to as the length and the width.

width

length

The length of this rectangle is 4 units and the width is 2 units. One way you can find the **area** of the rectangle is by counting the unit squares. There are 8 unit squares, so the area is 8 square units.

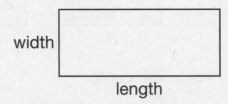

2 units

4 units

Another way to find the area is to multiply the length by its width.

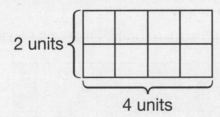

length   width   Area

4   ×   2   =   8

The area is the same using both methods, but using multiplication is usually quicker.

Example 1

Find the area of the rectangle.

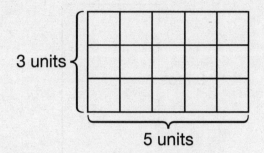

3 units

5 units

Strategy   Multiply the side lengths to find the area.

Step 1   Determine the length and width of the rectangle.

   The length of the rectangle is 5 units.
   The width is 3 units.

Step 2   Find the area of the rectangle.

   Multiply the length of the rectangle by its width.

   length   width   Area
    5   ×   3   =   15

Solution   The area of the rectangle is 15 square units.

Example 2

Ms. Walker bought a new rug for her living room. What is the area of the rug?

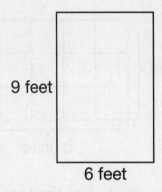

9 feet

6 feet

Strategy   Multiply the side lengths to find the area.

> **Step 1**   Determine the length and width of the rug.
>
> The rug is in the shape of a rectangle.
> The length of the rug is 6 feet. The width is 9 feet.

> **Step 2**   Find the area of the rug.
>
> Multiply the length of the rug by its width.
>
> $6 \times 9 = 54$
>
> The rug is measured in feet.

Solution   The area of the rug is 54 square feet.

The **distributive property of multiplication** allows you to break a factor into a sum. Multiply the other factor by each addend to find the final product.

To find the product of 8×9, you can break apart the factor 9 into $5 + 4$.

$8 \times 9 = 8 \times (5 + 4)$

Multiply 8 by each addend, and then add the products.

$8 \times (5 + 4) = (8 \times 5) + (8 \times 4)$

$= 40 + 32$

$= 72$

So, $8 \times 9 = 72$.

Example 3

Find the area of the rectangle.

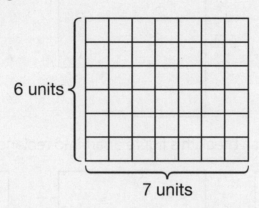

Strategy   Use the distributive property.

Step 1   Break apart the length of the rectangle into two addends.

       The length of the rectangle is 7 units. Break 7 into 5 + 2.

       Draw a line to separate 7 units into 5 units and 2 units.

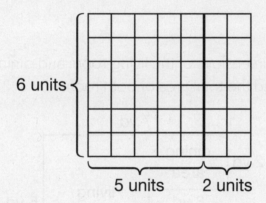

Step 2   Multiply the side lengths.

       The length of the rectangle is (5 + 2) units. The width is 6 units.

       Multiply using the distributive property.

$$(5 + 2) \times 6 = (5 \times 6) + (2 \times 6)$$
$$= 30 + 12$$
$$= 42$$

Solution   The area of the rectangle is 42 square inches.

Some figures can be broken apart into two or more rectangles.

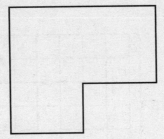

Here are three ways you can break this figure apart into rectangles.

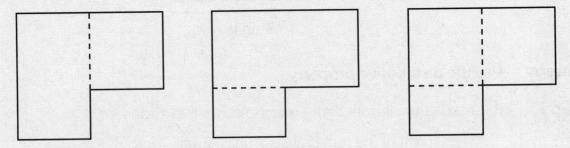

The area of each part can be added to find the area of the entire figure.

Example 4

The diagram shows the dimensions of the living room and dining area of Mr. Klein's apartment. Find the total area of both rooms.

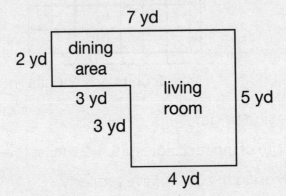

Strategy   Break the figure apart into rectangles to find the total area.

Step 1 Break the figure apart into two rectangles that do not overlap.

Draw a line on the figure to form two rectangles.
The dining area has a length of 3 yards and a width of 2 yards.
The living room has a length of 5 yards and a width of 4 yards.

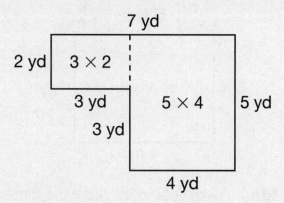

Step 2 Find the area of each room.

Area of dining area

$3 \times 2 = 6$ square yards

Area of living room

$5 \times 4 = 20$ square yards

Step 3 Add the areas.

$6 + 20 = 26$ square yards

Solution The total area of both rooms is 26 square yards.

The diagram shows the dimensions of Cheyenne's bedroom and closet.
Find the total area of the bedroom and closet.

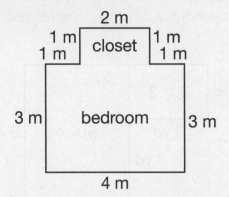

Draw a line on the figure to form two rectangles. Label the dimensions of the rectangles formed.

The closet has a length of _____ meters and a width of _____ meter.

The bedroom has a length of _____ meters and a width of _____ meters.

Find the area of each room.

Closet

_____ × _____ = _____

The area of the closet is _____ square meters.

Bedroom

_____ × _____ = _____

The area of the bedroom is _____ square meters.

Add to find the total area.

_____ + _____ = _____

The total area of the bedroom and closet is _____ square meters.

1 Look at the measurements for each length and width of a rectangle.
Is the area of the rectangle equal to 20 square units? Select Yes or No.

A. length = 5 units, width = 4 units   ○ Yes   ○ No

B. length = 5 units, width = 5 units   ○ Yes   ○ No

C. length = 10 units, width = 2 units   ○ Yes   ○ No

D. length = 10 units, width = 10 units   ○ Yes   ○ No

2 Cody says these two figures have the same area. Is he correct?
Use words, numbers, or models to explain your answer.

4 units

9 units

6 units

6 units

3 Which is a way that James can use to find the total area of the figure? Mark all that apply.

- ○ **A.** $(6 \times 3) + (7 \times 3)$
- ○ **B.** $(6 \times 3) + (7 \times 4)$
- ○ **C.** $(4 \times 3) + (6 \times 3)$
- ○ **D.** $(3 \times 3) + (7 \times 3)$
- ○ **E.** $(3 \times 4) + (6 \times 3) + (4 \times 3)$

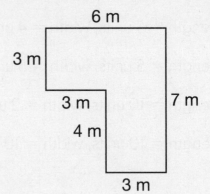

4 Draw a line from each figure to its area.

A. 1 ft [rectangle] 6 ft

•

• 9 square feet

B. 4 ft [rectangle] 2 ft

•

• 8 square feet

C. 3 ft [square] 3 ft

•

• 7 square feet

D. 2 ft 2 ft 1 ft 3 ft [figure] 1 ft 5 ft

•

• 6 square feet

5 Alejandro divided his garden into 4 equal sections. Each section is 5 feet long and 3 feet wide.

What is the area of one section of the garden? _____ square feet

What is the total area of the garden? _____ square feet

6 Complete the table to find the missing side lengths or area.

Figure	Length (units)	Width (units)	Area (square units)
Rectangle A	5	2	
Rectangle B		6	42
Rectangle C	9		27

7 Use numbers from the box to complete the equation to find the area of the rectangle.

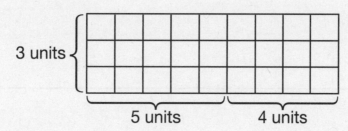

3 units

5 units   4 units

$3 \times (5 + 4) = ($ _____ $\times$ _____ $) + ($ _____ $\times$ _____ $)$

3

4

5

9

8 Megan set up two tables at the arts and crafts show to display her work. The diagram shows the identical tables Megan set up.

Break apart each table into different pairs of rectangles. Find the total area of each table.

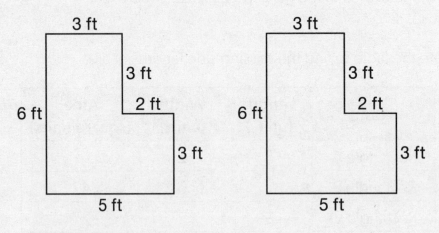

9 A rectangle has a length of 6 units and a width of 3 units. Hannah says the perimeter of the rectangle is 18 units. James says the area of the rectangle is 18 square units. Who is correct? Use words, numbers, or models to explain your answer.

10 Alicia and Tyrell both draw a rectangle with a length of 5 units and a width of 4 units.

Part A

Alicia adds 4 units to the width of the rectangle. She writes $5 \times (4 + 4)$ to represent the area of her new rectangle. On the grid, draw Alicia's rectangle. Label the length and the width.

Part B

Use the distributive property to write the area of Alicia's rectangle as the sum of two areas. Then find the area of the rectangle.

11 A square has a perimeter of 20 inches. Complete each statement.

The side length of the square is _____ inches.

The area of the square is _____ square inches.

Perimeter and Area of Rectangles

1 GETTING THE IDEA

Meg has a garden. The **perimeter** of the garden is 12 meters.

The **area** of the garden is 8 square meters.

Meg's Garden

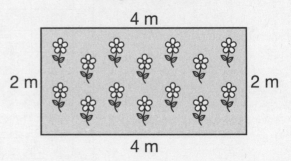

Meg drew two diagrams of the garden with the same perimeter but with a different area.

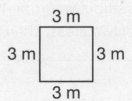

Perimeter = 5 + 1 + 5 + 1 = 12 meters

Area = 5 × 2 = 10 square meters

Perimeter = 3 + 3 + 3 + 3 = 12 meters

Area = 3 × 3 = 9 square meters

Meg drew another diagram of the garden with the same area but with a different perimeter.

Area = 1 × 8 = 8 square meters

Perimeter = 1 + 8 + 1 + 8 = 18 meters

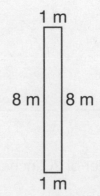

Example 1

This rectangle has a perimeter of 24 feet.

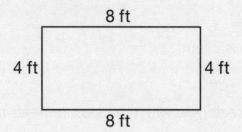

Draw another rectangle with the same perimeter. Use different side lengths.

Strategy **Change the length. Adjust the width to create a figure with the same perimeter.**

Step 1 Change the length.

The length of the rectangle is 8 feet.
Change it to another number.

The number 10 is an easy number to add mentally.
Use 10 feet for the length.

Step 2 Draw a rectangle. Label the new length.

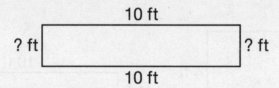

Perimeter = 10 ft + ? ft + 10 ft + ? ft

= 20 ft + ? ft

Step 3 Use the perimeter to find the unknown.

You want the perimeter to be 24 feet.

24 = 20 + ?

24 = 20 + 4

The unknown is 4 feet. That is the total measurement of two sides of the rectangle.

Step 4   Find the width.

Divide by 2 to find the width of one side.

$4 \div 2 = 2$

The width is 2 feet.

Step 5   Check your answer.

Label the rectangle with the measurements and find the perimeter.

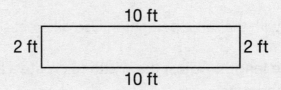

$10 + 2 + 10 + 2 = 24$

The perimeter is the same.

Solution   **The rectangle in Step 5 has the same perimeter of 24 feet.**

Example 2

These two rectangles have a perimeter of 24 feet. How do their areas compare?

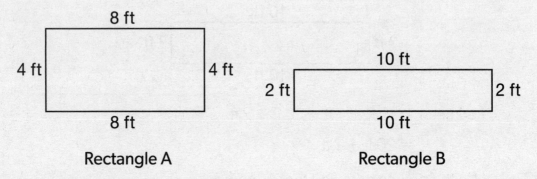

Rectangle A   **Rectangle B**

Strategy   **Multiply to find area.**

Step 1   Find the area of each rectangle.

area of rectangle A = 8 × 4 = 32   area of rectangle B = 10 × 2 = 20

The area is 32 square feet.   The area is 20 square feet.

Step 2 Compare the areas.

32 square feet > 20 square feet

Rectangle A has a greater area than Rectangle B.

These rectangles have the same perimeter, but they do not have the same area.

Solution **The area of Rectangle A is greater than the area of Rectangle B.**

Example 3

Aida drew this rectangle in her painting. The area of the rectangle is 40 square inches.

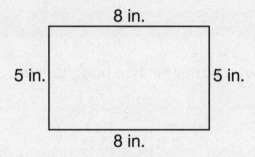

Draw a different rectangle with the same area, but a different perimeter.

Strategy **Think of other factors with a product of 40.**

Step 1 Find other numbers that have a product of 40.

The area has to be 40 square inches. So the product of the length and width must be 40.

What other factors have a product of 40?

$4 \times 10 = 40$

The length can be 10 inches, and the width can be 4 inches.

Step 2 Draw and label a rectangle with the new measurements.

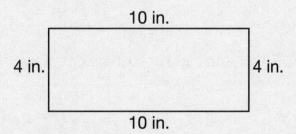

Step 3 Find the perimeter of the rectangle Aida drew.

perimeter = 8 + 5 + 8 + 5 = 26

The perimeter is 26 inches.

Step 4 Find the perimeter of the new rectangle.

perimeter = 10 + 4 + 10 + 4 = 28

The perimeter is 28 inches.

Solution A rectangle with the same area but different perimeter is shown in Step 2. It has the length of 10 inches and width of 4 inches.

② COACHED EXAMPLE

The rectangle below shows a poster Nathan bought. It has a perimeter of 10 feet.

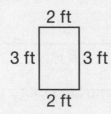

2 ft

3 ft   3 ft

2 ft

Draw a rectangle that has the same perimeter but a different area.

The perimeter must be _____ feet. Change one of the side lengths from Nathan's poster.

Make the length 4 feet.

Write the new perimeter equation with the new length.

10 = _____ + ? + _____ + ?

Find the unknown.

10 = _____ + ?

? = _____

The unknown is _____. That is the total measurement of two sides of the rectangle.

So, divide by 2 to find the width.

_____ ÷ 2 = _____

The width is _____ foot.

Draw the new rectangle. Label the measurements.

Find the area of Nathan's poster.

Area = _____ × _____

= _____

The area of Nathan's poster is _____ square feet.

Find the area of the new rectangle.

Area = _____ × _____

= _____

The area of the new rectangle is _____ square feet.

The new rectangle has a length of _____ feet and a width of _____ foot.

It has a perimeter of _____ and an area of _____.

1 Draw a line from each rectangle to the rectangle with the same area.

A. 6 in. 4 in. •   • 6 in. 6 in.

B. 9 in. 4 in. •   • 4 in. 5 in.

C. 3 in. 6 in. •   • 9 in. 2 in.

D. 2 in. 10 in. •   • 3 in. 8 in.

2 Draw 4 different rectangles that have a perimeter of 16 units.
Use only whole number units for lengths and widths.

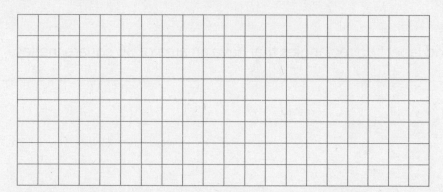

What are the dimensions of the rectangle with the greatest area? _____

What are the dimensions of the rectangle with the least area? _____

3 Miguel drew a square that measures 6 inches on each side.
Select True or False for each statement.

A. A rectangle that measures 12 inches   ○ True   ○ False
by 2 inches has the same area as
Miguel's square.

B. A rectangle that measures 10 inches   ○ True   ○ False
by 2 inches has the same perimeter as
Miguel's square.

C. There is no other square with the   ○ True   ○ False
same area as Miguel's square.

D. There is no other rectangle with   ○ True   ○ False
the same area as Miguel's square.

4 Zan is making patches for a quilt. She wants each patch to have an area of 36 square inches.

Part A

Draw and label two rectangles that have an area of 36 square inches.

Part B

Describe how you found the measurements for the rectangles you drew.

5 Joe drew a square. He says that there are many squares with the same area as his square. Beth says there are no other squares with the same area as Joe's square. Who is correct? Explain your reasoning. Draw an example to prove your reasoning.

6 Sophie drew a rectangle. It has a perimeter of 18 inches. Its area is 18 square inches. What are the length and width of the rectangle?

length = _____ inches

width = _____ inches

7 Chang is making a playpen for his puppy. It will be in the shape of a rectangle. He has 20 feet of fencing.

Part A

What are some of the measurements of the pen Chang could make?

Part B

Which pen will give his puppy the greatest area to run around in?

_____

8 Hilda wants a garden to have an area of 20 square feet. She will put a fence around the garden. What is the least amount of fencing she could use? Explain your answer using words, numbers, or drawings.

1 Students measured the lengths of ribbons to the nearest $\frac{1}{2}$ inch.

$2\frac{1}{2}$	2	$2\frac{1}{2}$	4	$3\frac{1}{2}$	3	$2\frac{1}{2}$	$2\frac{1}{2}$	3
$3\frac{1}{2}$	4	$2\frac{1}{2}$	3	$3\frac{1}{2}$	4	$2\frac{1}{2}$	$3\frac{1}{2}$	$3\frac{1}{2}$

Make a line plot of the data. Remember to include a title and label for the number line.

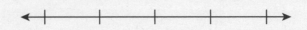

2 Aki poured water into the measuring cups.

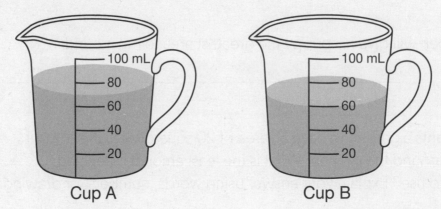

Cup A   Cup B

Use the numbers from the box to answer the questions.

What is the total liquid volume of the two cups?

_____ milliliters

How many more milliliters of water is in Cup A

than in Cup B? _____ milliliters

10
20
130
140
180
200

3 Compare the areas and perimeters of the figures. Write the letters of the figures in the correct box.

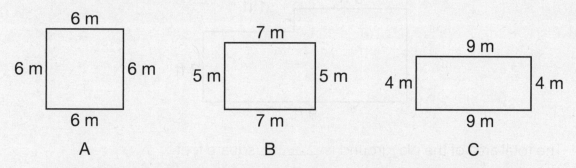

6 m
6 m 6 m
6 m
A

7 m
5 m 5 m
7 m
B

9 m
4 m 4 m
9 m
C

Same Area	Same Perimeter	Different Area and Different Perimeter
_____ and _____	_____ and _____	_____ and _____

4 Students voted on fun activities after school. The table and picture graph show the results. The key in the picture graph is missing.

Fun Activity	Number of Votes
Jump Rope	15
Play Hopscotch	10
Play Sports	30
Ride Bike	25

Fun Activity

Jump Rope	✓ ✓ ✓
Play Hopscotch	✓ ✓
Play Sports	✓ ✓ ✓ ✓ ✓ ✓
Ride Bike	✓ ✓ ✓ ✓ ✓

Key: Each ✓ = _____ votes

How many votes does each check mark stand for? _____ votes

Describe the strategy you used to find your answer.

5 A playground is shown in the diagram.

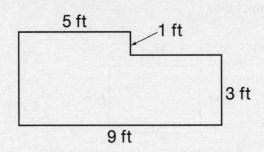

The total area of the playground is _____ square feet.

Explain how you found your answer.

6 Diego found three rocks on a hike. The mass of each rock is shown below.

Rock	Mass (in grams)
A	156
B	148
C	90

Which statement about the rocks is correct? Mark all that apply.

○ **A.** The total mass of Rock A and Rock B is 304 grams.

○ **B.** Five rocks with the same mass as Rock C would be 450 grams.

○ **C.** The mass of Rock C is 48 grams less than the mass of Rock B.

○ **D.** The combined mass of all three rocks is about 400 grams.

○ **E.** Two rocks with the same mass as Rock C have a mass that is less than the mass of Rock A.

7 Ms. Lin asked students which types of books they read last month. She made a bar graph of the data.

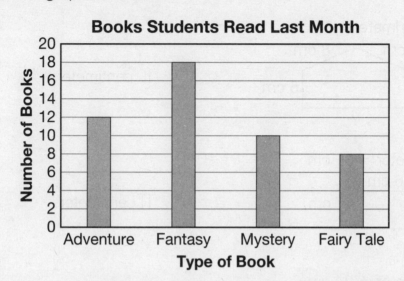

Books Students Read Last Month

Students read as many fantasy books as they did two other types of books combined. Which are the two types of books combined? Explain how you found your answer.

```
┌─────────────────────────────────────────────────┐
│                                                 │
│                                                 │
│                                                 │
│                                                 │
└─────────────────────────────────────────────────┘
```

8 Find the area of the rectangle. Use the numbers in the box to complete the equation and solve.

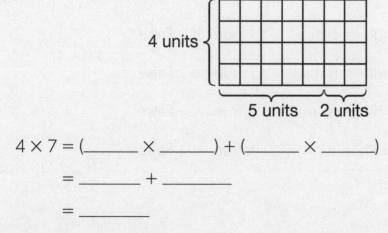

4 units

5 units   2 units

| 2 |
| 4 |
| 5 |
| 8 |
| 20 |
| 28 |

$4 \times 7 = ($ _____ $\times$ _____ $) + ($ _____ $\times$ _____ $)$

$\qquad = $ _____ $+$ _____

$\qquad = $ _____

The area of the rectangle is _____ square units.

9 Draw a line from each figure to the correct length of its unknown side.

A.
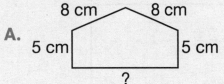
Perimeter = 37 cm
8 cm   8 cm
5 cm   5 cm
?

• 10 centimeters

B.
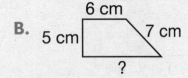
Perimeter = 31 cm
6 cm
5 cm   7 cm
?

• 11 centimeters

C.
Perimeter = 24 cm
6 cm   ?
8 cm

• 12 centimeters

D.
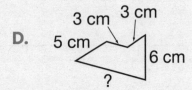
Perimeter = 29 cm
3 cm 3 cm
5 cm
6 cm
?

• 13 centimeters

10 Is the area of the rectangle 40 square meters? Select True or False.

A. length = 8 m, width = 5 m   ○ True   ○ False

B. length = 7 m, width = 6 m   ○ True   ○ False

C. length = 4 m, width = 10 m   ○ True   ○ False

D. length = 2 m, width = 10 m   ○ True   ○ False

11 An activity book has some mazes.

- Matt started the mazes at 9:16 and finished at 9:43.
- Jeannie started the mazes at 11:12 and finished at 11:41.
- Katie started the mazes at 10:15 and finished 27 minutes later.

Using the information above, is the statement true? Select Yes or No.

A. Jeannie did the mazes faster than Matt.   ○ Yes   ○ No

B. Matt finished in the same amount of time as Katie.   ○ Yes   ○ No

C. Katie finished at 10:42.   ○ Yes   ○ No

D. It took Jeannie 39 minutes to finish the mazes.   ○ Yes   ○ No

Lucia drew the rectangle below. Use the rectangle for problems 12–13.

= 1 square inch

12 Explain why the labeled square can be called a unit square. How can Lucia use the unit squares to measure the area of the rectangle?

13 Find the area of the rectangle.

The area of the rectangle is _____ square inches.

ART PROJECT

The art teacher, Mr. McCall, needs to purchase supplies for a class project. He needs to buy paintbrushes, paint, and art canvases.

For the project, each student will paint one square canvas. The square canvas has a side length of 1 foot. Mr. McCall will sew the canvases together, without gaps or overlaps, to make one large class project.

Part A The table shows how many paintbrushes of different widths are needed. Display the data on a line plot. How many total paintbrushes will Mr. McCall buy?

Width of Brushes (in inches)	$\frac{1}{4}$	$\frac{2}{4}$	$\frac{3}{4}$	1	$1\frac{1}{4}$	$1\frac{2}{4}$	$1\frac{3}{4}$	2
Number of Brushes	5	4	5	6	3	4	2	1

Part B The bar graph shows how much of each color paint is needed to complete the project.

Paint is sold in large jars of 250 milliliters and small jars of 100 milliliters. How many small and large jars should Mr. McCall buy of each color? How much paint is needed in all to complete the project?

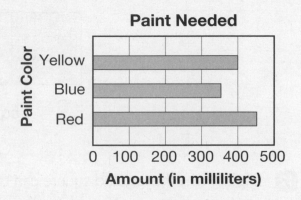

Part C There are 24 students in Mr. McCall's art class. After each student paints one square canvas, Mr. McCall will sew them together. What will be the area of the combined canvases? Explain your answer.

Part D Draw two ways Mr. McCall could combine the square canvases together to make one rectangular canvas.
• Label the length and width of each rectangle. Show that the area is the same for both.
• Find the perimeter for each rectangular canvas you drew. Show your work.

DOMAIN 5

Geometry

Two-Dimensional Shapes

1 GETTING THE IDEA

A **polygon** is a closed figure. It has three or more straight sides. The figures below are polygons because their sides are straight and they are closed figures.

Polygons

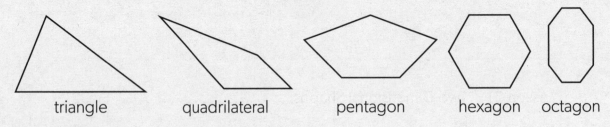

| triangle | quadrilateral | pentagon | hexagon | octagon |

A circle is **not** a polygon. It is a closed figure, but it does not have straight sides.

Example 1

Which figure is a polygon? Select all that apply.

A.   B.   C.   D.

Strategy   Use the definition of polygon.

Step 1   Remember the properties of a polygon.

A polygon is a closed figure.

It has three or more straight sides.

Step 2   Identify the figures that are closed.

Figures A, C, and D are closed figures.

Figure B is **not** closed. It has a gap between two sides.

Step 3   Identify the closed figures that have straight sides.

All the sides of Figures A and C are line segments.

Figure D is not a polygon. It is curved.

Solution   Figures A and C are polygons.

Polygons are named by the number of sides they have. A **quadrilateral** is a polygon with four sides and four **angles**.

Example 2

Identify each figure as a quadrilateral or not a quadrilateral. Write the figure in the correct box.

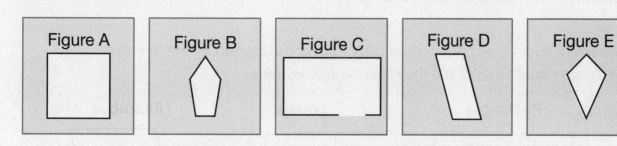

Quadrilateral	Not a Quadrilateral

Strategy   Use the definition of quadrilateral.

Step 1   Remember the properties of a quadrilateral.

A quadrilateral is a polygon with 4 sides.

Step 2 Determine if each figure has the properties of a quadrilateral.

Figure A is a closed figure with four sides. It is a quadrilateral.

Figure B is a closed figure with five sides. It is not a quadrilateral.

Figure C is not a closed figure. So it cannot be a quadrilateral.

Figure D is a closed figure with four sides. It is a quadrilateral.

Figure E is a closed figure with four sides. It is a quadrilateral.

Step 3 Complete the table.

Quadrilateral	Not a Quadrilateral
Figure A Figure D Figure E	Figure B Figure C

Solution The table is shown in Step 3.

There are different types of quadrilaterals. They are identified by the length of their sides and whether or not they have square corners.

Rectangle   **Square**   **Rhombus**

- Two pairs of opposite sides that are the same length
- Four square corners

- Four sides that are the same length
- Four square corners

- Four sides that are the same length

Example 3

Describe the figure below in more than one way. Use the names *quadrilateral*, *rectangle*, *square*, and *rhombus*.

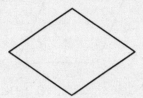

Strategy   Look at the sides and angles of the figure.

Step 1   Count the sides of the figure.

The figure has four sides. It is a quadrilateral.

Step 2   Compare the sides of the figure.

All four sides of the figure appear to be the same length.

The figure is a rhombus.

Step 3   Look at the corners of the figure.

The angles are not square corners, so the figure cannot be a square.

Solution   The figure is a *quadrilateral* and a *rhombus*.

Example 4

Draw two quadrilaterals that are not rectangles.

Strategy   Use the properties of a rectangle.

Step 1   Describe the properties of a rectangle.

A rectangle has two pairs of opposite sides that are the same length.

It has four square corners.

Step 2   Describe a quadrilateral that does not have the properties of a rectangle.

The quadrilateral may or may not have two pairs of opposite sides that are the same length.

It does not have four square corners.

Step 3 Draw two quadrilaterals to match the description in Step 2.

This quadrilateral does not have four square corners.

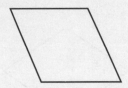

This quadrilateral does not have 2 pairs of opposite sides that are the same length.

It has only 1 square corner.

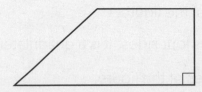

Solution A rhombus and a trapezoid are quadrilaterals that are not rectangles.

② COACHED EXAMPLE

Draw a square. Then draw a rhombus that is not a square. Explain how the figures are the same and how they are different.

Square   Rhombus

Both figures have _____ sides that are the same _____.

The square has _____ square corners. The rhombus has _____ square corners.

1 Identify each figure as a polygon or not a polygon. Write the letters of the figures in the correct box.

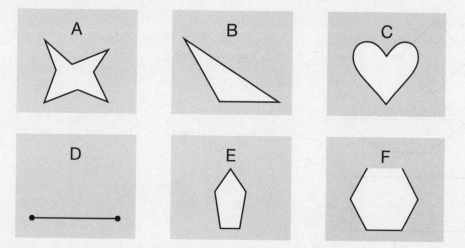

Polygon	Not a Polygon

2 What is the name of the figure shown? Mark all that apply.

○ **A.** quadrilateral
○ **B.** rectangle
○ **C.** rhombus
○ **D.** square

3 Fill in the blanks to explain what kind of figure is shown.

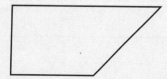

This figure is a quadrilateral because it has ____ sides.

It is not a _____ or a _____ because it has only

two square corners.

4 Carmen drew a rectangle. Is each figure one that Carmen could have drawn? Select Yes or No.

A. 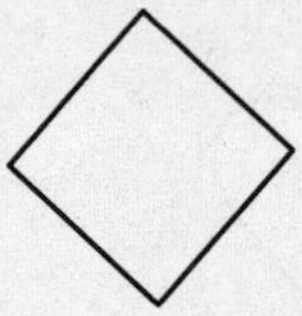 ○ Yes ○ No

B.  ○ Yes ○ No

C. 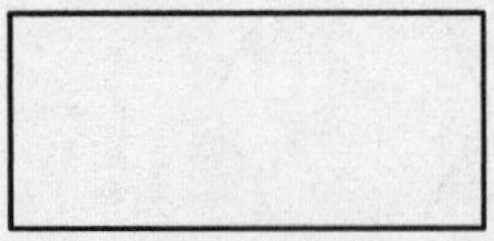 ○ Yes ○ No

D. 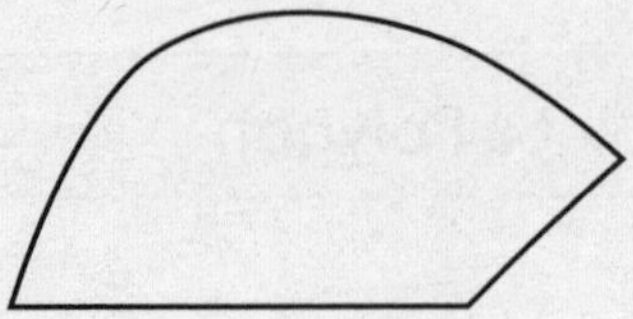 ○ Yes ○ No

E.  ○ Yes ○ No

F.  ○ Yes ○ No

5 Draw a rectangle that is also a square. Explain how you know that your drawing is correct.

6 Clay and Dana both looked at the figure below.

- Clay said that it is a rhombus.
- Dana said that it is a square.

Who is correct? _____

Explain your answer.

```
[                                                                    ]
```

7 Select True or False for each statement about the figures shown.

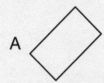 A

 B

 C

 D

 E

 F

A. All of the figures are quadrilaterals.   ○ True   ○ False

B. All of the figures are polygons.   ○ True   ○ False

C. Figures B, C, and D are rectangles.   ○ True   ○ False

D. Figures B and F are rhombuses.   ○ True   ○ False

E. Figures A and F are rectangles.   ○ True   ○ False

8 **Part A**

Draw a rhombus and a quadrilateral that does **not** have square corners.

Part B

Explain how your quadrilaterals are similar.

Part C

Explain how your quadrilaterals are different.

9 Derek drew a polygon with four straight sides. He said that it was **not** a rhombus, a rectangle, or a square.

Part A

Draw a figure that Derek could have drawn.

Part B

Explain why the figure you drew is **not** a rhombus, a rectangle, or a square.

Part C

Name the figure you drew. Use as many different names as possible.

_____

LESSON 32

Equal Areas

1 GETTING THE IDEA

Area is the measure of the amount of space that covers a figure. Area is measured in square units. The shading in the figure below shows the area of the square.

You can divide a shape into equal parts. Then you can name each part of the shape with a **unit fraction**.

The line divides the square into 2 equal parts with the same area.

Each part is $\frac{1}{2}$ of the square, so the area of each part is $\frac{1}{2}$ the area of the square.

Example 1

This rectangle is divided into equal parts.

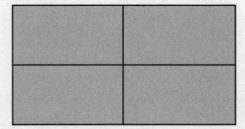

What fraction names each part of the rectangle?

Strategy Write a unit fraction.

Step 1   Write the numerator of the fraction.

         When you divide a figure into equal parts, each part is a unit fraction.

         The numerator of a unit fraction is 1.

$$\frac{1}{\square} \rightarrow \text{Each part is 1 part of the rectangle.}$$

Step 2   Write the denominator of the fraction.

         Count the total number of equal parts.

$$\frac{1}{4} \rightarrow \text{There are 4 equal parts.}$$

Solution   Each part of the rectangle is $\frac{1}{4}$ of the rectangle.

Example 2

What fraction describes the area of the shaded part of this square?

Strategy   **Write a unit fraction to describe the shaded part.**

Step 1   Look at the area of the shape.

         The area of the shape is the whole square.

Step 2   Write the numerator of the fraction.

         The numerator of a unit fraction is 1.

$$\frac{1}{\square} \rightarrow \text{Each part is 1 part of the square.}$$

Step 3 Write the denominator of the fraction.

Count the total number of equal parts.

$\frac{1}{3}$ → There are 3 equal parts.

Solution The area of the shaded part is $\frac{1}{3}$ the area of the whole square.

Example 3

The circle below is divided into equal parts. Which fraction describes the area of each part of this circle?

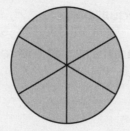

A. $\frac{1}{3}$

B. $\frac{1}{5}$

C. $\frac{1}{6}$

D. $\frac{1}{8}$

Strategy Determine the correct fraction.

Step 1 Write the numerator of the fraction.

If the parts of a figure are all equal, the area of each part is a unit fraction.

The numerator of a unit fraction is 1.

$\frac{1}{\boxed{}}$ → Each part is 1 part of the circle.

Step 2   Write the denominator of the fraction.

Count the total number of equal parts.

$\frac{1}{6}$ → There are 6 equal parts.

Solution   The fraction in Choice C, $\frac{1}{6}$, describes the area of each part of this circle.

Example 4

Shade the figure to show one part is $\frac{1}{5}$ the area of the rectangle.

Strategy   Use reasoning.

Step 1   Draw lines to divide the rectangle into 5 equal parts.

Step 2   Think about the meaning of $\frac{1}{5}$.

$\frac{1}{5}$ → 1 part to be shaded
$\phantom{\frac{1}{5}}$ → 5 equal parts in all

Step 3   Shade the figure.

Solution   The figure is shown in Step 3.

What fraction describes the area of each part of this figure?

Are the parts in the rectangle equal? _____

If they are, you may determine the area of each part.

Write a numerator.

If the parts of figure are equal, the area of each part is a _____ fraction.

Unit fractions have a _____ of 1.

The numerator of this fraction is _____.

Write a denominator.

The denominator is the number of _____ parts in all.

The figure has ____ equal parts.

The denominator is _____.

Write the fraction. $\dfrac{\square}{\square}$

The fraction $\dfrac{\square}{\square}$ describes the area of each part of the figure.

1 Draw a line from each figure to the fraction that describes the area of each part of the figure.

A.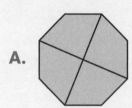

•   • $\frac{1}{2}$

B.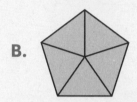

•   • $\frac{1}{4}$

C.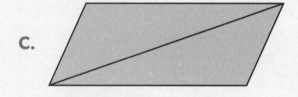

•   • $\frac{1}{5}$

D.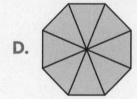

•   • $\frac{1}{8}$

2 Look at the shape on the right. Select True or False for each statement.

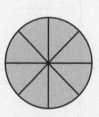

A. The shape is divided into equal parts.　　　　○ True　○ False

B. Each part is $\frac{1}{8}$ of the whole shape.　　　　○ True　○ False

C. The whole shape is represented by the fraction $\frac{8}{1}$.　　○ True　○ False

D. The area of each part is $\frac{1}{8}$ of the area of the whole shape.　　○ True　○ False

3 Bess drew a shape and divided it into parts. Each part is $\frac{1}{5}$ of the whole shape. Which could be Bess's drawing? Mark all that apply.

○ **A.**

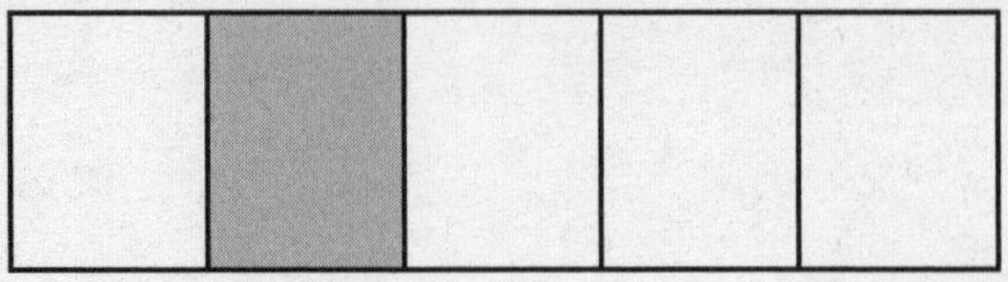

○ **B.**

○ **C.**

○ **D.**

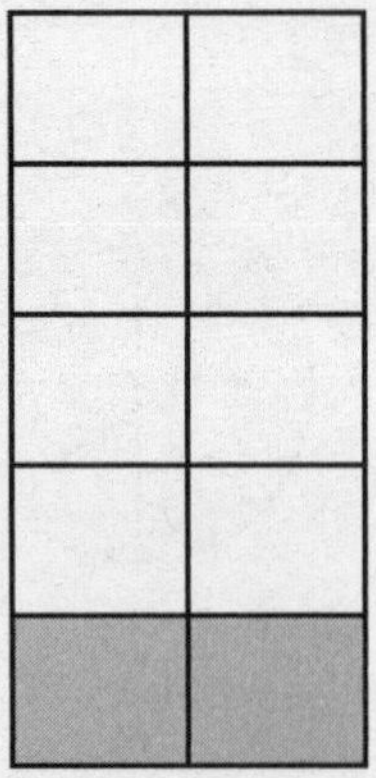

○ **E.**

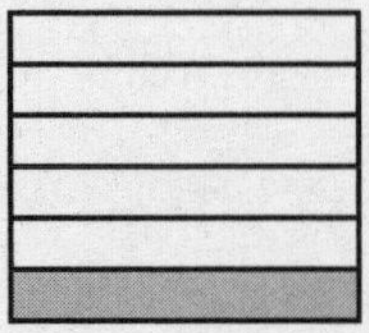

4 Draw lines to divide the square into 4 equal parts. Write a fraction to describe the area of each part of the square.

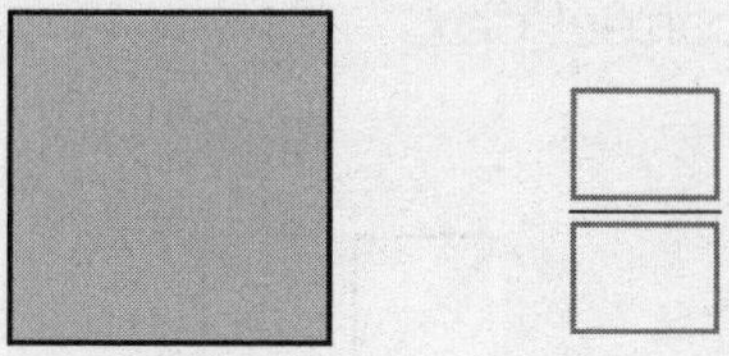

5 Theo drew a shape and shaded part of it. The area of the shaded part is $\frac{1}{3}$ of the area of the whole shape. Could each figure be Theo's drawing? Select Yes or No.

A. 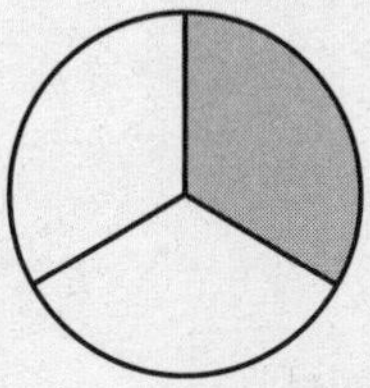 ○ Yes ○ No

B. 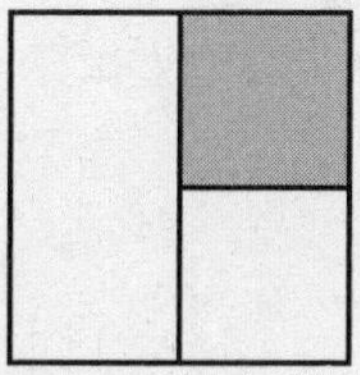 ○ Yes ○ No

C. 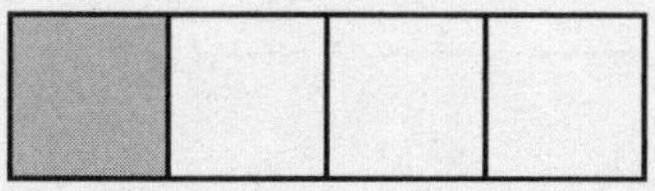 ○ Yes ○ No

D. 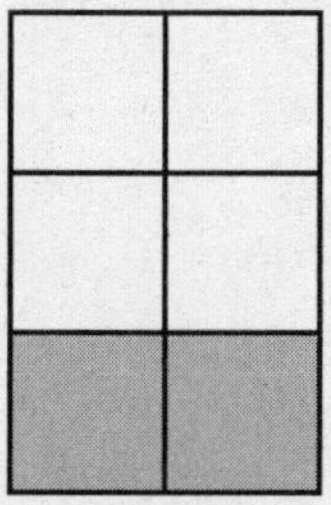 ○ Yes ○ No

E. 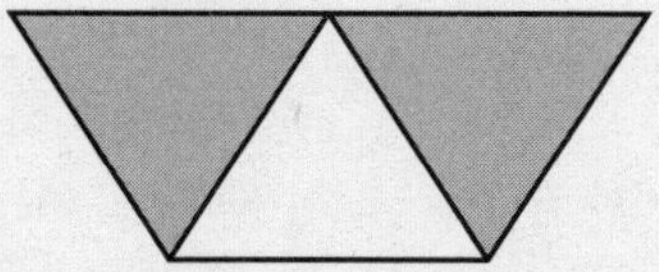 ○ Yes ○ No

6 Look at each shape. Decide whether each part of it has an area that is greater than or less than $\frac{1}{4}$ of the area of the whole shape. Write the letter of the shape in the correct box.

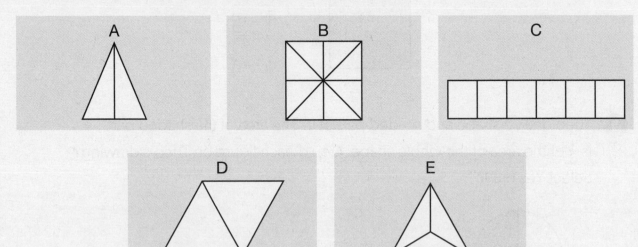

Area Greater Than $\frac{1}{4}$	Area Less Than $\frac{1}{4}$

7 Tomas drew part of a shape on the grid paper below. The part he drew is $\frac{1}{4}$ of the area of what he wanted the whole shape to be.

Draw a shape that Tomas might draw.

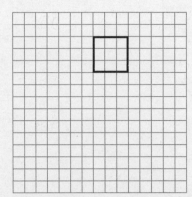

8 Franco and Myra each drew a rectangle on a grid. They each wrote a fraction that shows the part of the area of the whole rectangle.

Franco

Myra

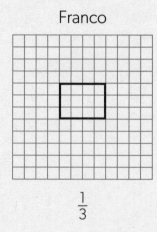

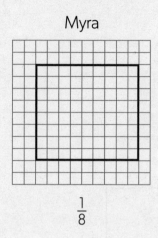

$\frac{1}{3}$

$\frac{1}{8}$

- Franco said his fraction of the area of the rectangle is greater than the fraction of the area of Myra's rectangle.

- Myra said her fraction of the area of the rectangle is greater than the fraction of the area of Franco's rectangle.

Part A

Who is correct?

_____

Part B

Explain your reasoning.

1 Does the shaded part of each figure represent $\frac{1}{2}$ of the total area? Select Yes or No.

A. 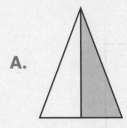 ○ Yes ○ No

B. 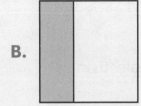 ○ Yes ○ No

C. 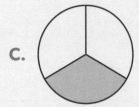 ○ Yes ○ No

D. 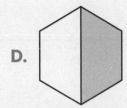 ○ Yes ○ No

2 Mika drew a quadrilateral. It has no square corners. Which could be the figure that Mika drew? Mark all that apply.

○ **A.** triangle   ○ **D.** rhombus

○ **B.** pentagon   ○ **E.** square

○ **C.** rectangle   ○ **F.** circle

3 Is the figure a quadrilateral? Write the letters of the figures in the correct box.

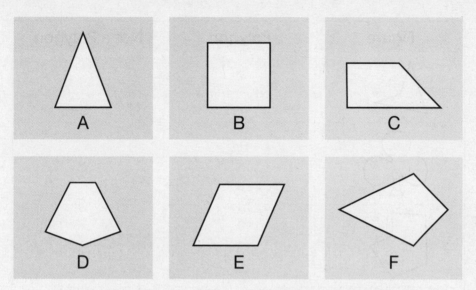

Quadrilateral	Not a Quadrilateral

4 Use the words from the box to name the figure in three ways.

quadrilateral
circle
rectangle
triangle
rhombus
square
polygon

_____

_____

_____

5 Write an "X" to show whether the figure is a polygon or not a polygon.

Figure	Polygon	Not a Polygon

6 Lexi drew the figure below. Select True or False for each statement.

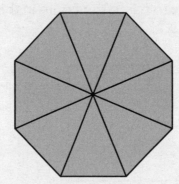

A. Lexi divided the figure into equal parts. ○ True ○ False

B. Each part of the figure is $\frac{8}{8}$. ○ True ○ False

C. The total area of the figure is $\frac{1}{8}$. ○ True ○ False

D. Each part of the figure is $\frac{1}{8}$ of the area of the figure. ○ True ○ False

7 Divide the square into 3 equal parts.

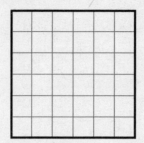

Write a fraction that names each equal part. _____

8 Draw a line from each figure to the unit fraction that describes the area of each part of the figure.

A. •   • $\frac{1}{8}$

B. •   • $\frac{1}{6}$

C. •   • $\frac{1}{4}$

D. •   • $\frac{1}{3}$

9 Select True or False for each statement.

    A. All quadrilaterals are polygons.   ○ True   ○ False

    B. All polygons are quadrilaterals.   ○ True   ○ False

    C. All rectangles are squares.   ○ True   ○ False

    D. All squares are rhombuses.   ○ True   ○ False

10 Mr. Banks drew two different figures on the board.

- Both figures were quadrilaterals.

- Both had four square corners.

- One has all sides the same length.

Part A

Draw two figures that could match the figures Mr. Banks drew. Use the grid.

Part B

Name the figures that you drew. Explain why you know that both figures are correct.

11 **Part A**

Draw a rhombus and a rectangle. Label each figure.

```
┌─────────────────────────────────────────────────────────┐
│                                                         │
│                                                         │
│                                                         │
│                                                         │
│                                                         │
│                                                         │
└─────────────────────────────────────────────────────────┘
```

Part B

Describe two ways that the figures are alike.

```
┌─────────────────────────────────────────────────────────┐
│                                                         │
│                                                         │
│                                                         │
│                                                         │
└─────────────────────────────────────────────────────────┘
```

Part C

Describe two ways that the figures are different.

```
┌─────────────────────────────────────────────────────────┐
│                                                         │
│                                                         │
│                                                         │
│                                                         │
└─────────────────────────────────────────────────────────┘
```

12 Shade each figure to represent one part of the area of the whole. Then write the unit fraction that represents the shaded part of the figure.

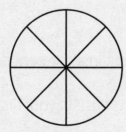 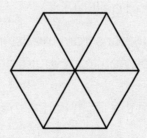

_____   _____

DESIGN A QUILT B L O C K

Your class is making a quilt of square blocks. Each student will design two quilt blocks. All of the quilt blocks will be sewn together and will hang on a wall in your classroom.

Part A Design your first quilt block. Each block should be made of polygons that do not overlap or have gaps between them. Use at least three of the polygons listed below. You can also use other polygons as well. Then list the polygons you used in the first quilt block.

- a triangle whose area is $\frac{1}{2}$ of the area of the whole block

- a square whose area is $\frac{1}{4}$ of the area of the whole block

- a rectangle that is not a square

- a rhombus that is not a square

Part B In the first column of the chart below, write the name of each quadrilateral used in your first block. In the next three columns, place an "✗" under all the properties for that quadrilateral.

Quadrilateral	2 Pairs of Opposite Sides the Same Length	4 Sides the Same Length	4 Square Corners

Part C Design a second block that follows the rules listed below. Then list the polygons you used in the second quilt block.

- Use at least two polygons from the list in Part A.
- When you use a polygon from your first block, put it in a different place in your second block.
- Use a polygon from the list in Part A that you did not use in your first block.

Part D How do you know that the rectangle and rhombus used in your quilt blocks are not squares?

GLOSSARY

addend any number that is added in addition (Lessons 12, 13)

$$7 + 3 = 10$$

angle where two sides meet in a figure (Lesson 31)

A rectangle has 4 angles.

area the measure of a figure or surface in square units (Lessons 28, 29, 30, 32)

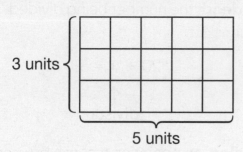

3 units

5 units

area = 15 square units

area model a rectangular model made of square tiles (Lessons 1, 2, 3, 4)

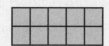

array a set of objects arranged in rows that each have the same number of objects (Lessons 1, 2, 3, 4)

3 rows with 4 circles in each row

associative property of addition the property that states that the addends can be grouped in different ways and the sum will be the same (Lesson 12)

$$18 + (12 + 5) = (18 + 12) + 5$$

associative property of multiplication the property that states that the factors can be grouped in different ways and the product will be the same (Lessons 6, 15)

$$2 \times (5 \times 7) = (2 \times 5) \times 7$$

bar graph a graph that uses horizontal or vertical bars to show data (Lesson 25)

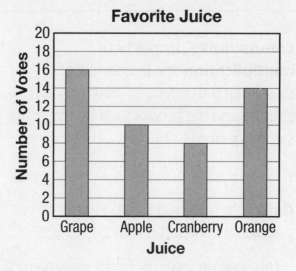

benchmark a known amount used to make comparisons (Lessons 22, 23)

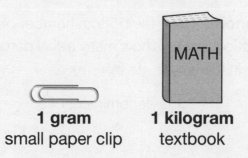

1 gram
small paper clip

1 kilogram
textbook

capacity the amount a container can hold (Lesson 23)

This bucket has a capacity of 10 liters.

commutative property of addition the property that states that the order of the addends can change and the sum will be the same (Lessons 9, 12)

$$17 + 12 = 12 + 17$$

commutative property of multiplication the property that states that the order of the factors can change and the product will be the same (Lessons 6, 15)

$$2 \times 3 = 3 \times 2$$

data information collected about people or things (Lessons 24, 25, 26)

The ages, in years, of Sara's classmates are: 7, 8, 8, 6, 9, 7, 9, 8, 7, 7, 8, 8, 7, 8, 8, 9, 8, 7, 9, 9.

denominator the bottom number of a fraction that tells how many equal parts are in the whole (Lesson 16)

$\frac{2}{3}$ has a denominator of 3

difference the result of a subtraction problem (Lesson 14)

$$12 - 7 = 5$$
↑
difference

distributive property of multiplication the property that states that multiplying a sum by a number is the same as multiplying each addend by the number and then adding the products (Lessons 6, 12, 29)

$$32 + 12 = 4 \times 8 + 4 \times 3$$
$$= 4 \times (8 + 3)$$

dividend the number being divided (Lessons 4, 5)

$$20 \div 4 = 5$$
↑
divisor

division an operation that can be used to find the number of equal groups or the number of objects in each group (Lesson 2)

When 10 books are divided into 2 equal piles, there are 5 books in each pile.

$$10 \div 2 = 5$$

divisor the number by which another number is divided (Lessons 4, 5)

$$18 \div 3 = 6$$
↑
divisor

elapsed time the amount of time that passes from the beginning to the end of an activity (Lesson 21)

The elapsed time is 16 minutes.

equal groups two or more groups that have the same number of objects (Lessons 1, 3, 4)

equation a number sentence that shows that the values on both sides of the equal sign are the same (Lessons 3, 4, 8)

$$2 + 3 = 5$$

equivalent fractions two or more fractions that name the same part or amount but have different numerators and denominators (Lessons 18, 19)

$$\frac{1}{2} = \frac{2}{4} = \frac{4}{8}$$

estimate to find about how many or about how much using a benchmark (Lessons 22, 23)

A book has a mass of about 1 kilogram.

even number a whole number that has a 0, 2, 4, 6, or 8 in the ones place (Lesson 9)

16 is an even number.

expanded form a way of writing a number as a sum of the values of its digits (Lesson 10)

8,211 in expanded form is 8,000 + 200 + 10 + 2.

factor a number multiplied by another number to find a product (Lessons 1, 5)

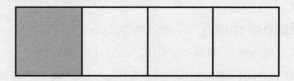

fraction a number that names part of a whole or part of a group (Lesson 16)

1 out of 4 equal parts is shaded.
$\frac{1}{4}$, or one fourth

gram (g) a metric unit of measure for mass (Lesson 22)

1,000 gram = 1 kilogram

hour (hr) a unit of time (Lesson 21)

$$1 \text{ hour} = 60 \text{ minutes}$$

inverse operations two operations that can be used to undo one another, such as addition and subtraction or multiplication and division (Lessons 5, 14)

$$6 + 3 = 9$$
$$9 - 3 = 6$$

is equal to (=) a symbol used to compare two numbers that means the first number is equal to the second number (Lesson 20)

$$212 = 212$$

212 is equal to 212.

is greater than (>) a symbol used to compare two numbers that means the first number is more than the second number (Lesson 20)

$$12 > 7$$

12 is greater than 7.

is less than (<) a symbol used to compare two numbers that means the first number is not as many as the second number (Lesson 20)

$$6 < 8$$

6 is less than 8.

key the part of a picture graph that tells how much each picture stands for (Lesson 24)

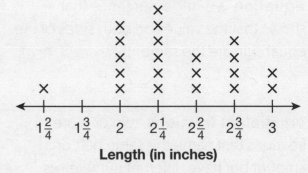

Number of Apples Picked

Ling	🍎 🍎 🍎
Grace	🍎 🍎 🍎 🍎
Jose	🍎 🍎
Kevin	🍎 🍎 🍎

Key: Each 🍎 = 2 apples

↑
KEY

kilogram (kg) a metric unit of measure for mass (Lesson 22)

$$1 \text{ kilogram} = 1{,}000 \text{ grams}$$

line plot a graph that shows data on a number line (Lesson 26)

Name Lengths

```
                    ×
        ×           ×
        ×           ×                   ×
        ×           ×           ×       ×
        ×           ×           ×       ×       ×
×       ×           ×           ×       ×       ×
←───┼───┼───┼───┼───┼───┼───┼───→
   1 2/4 1 3/4   2  2 1/4 2 2/4 2 3/4   3
```

Length (in inches)

liquid volume the capacity of a container or the amount of liquid a container can hold (Lesson 23)

When this bucket is filled with water, the liquid volume is 10 liters.

liter (L) a metric unit of measure for capacity (Lesson 23)

$$1 \text{ L} = 1{,}000 \text{ mL}$$

mass a metric unit of measure for the amount of matter in an object (Lesson 22)

A paper clip has a mass of about 1 gram.

A book has a mass of about 1 kilogram.

milliliter (mL) a metric unit of measure for capacity (Lesson 23)

$$1{,}000 \text{ mL} = 1 \text{ L}$$

minuend the number being subtracted from (Lesson 14)

$$15 - 7 = 8$$
↑
minuend

minute (min) a unit of time (Lesson 21)

60 minutes = 1 hour

multiple a number that is the product of two counting numbers (Lesson 15)

The multiples of 4 are 4, 8, 12, 16, 20, . . .

multiple of 10 a number that is the product of 10 and a counting number (Lesson 15)

The multiples of 10 are 10, 100, 1,000, 10,000, . . .

multiplication an operation that joins equal groups (Lesson 1)

4 rows of 7 counters each is 28 counters in all.

$$4 \times 7 = 28$$

numerator the top number of a fraction that tells how many equal parts of the whole are shaded or counted (Lesson 16)

$\frac{5}{8}$ has a numerator of 5.

odd number a whole number that has a 1, 3, 5, 7, or 9 in the ones place (Lesson 9)

61 is an odd number.

pattern an ordered set of numbers, shapes, or objects (Lesson 9)

$$+3 \quad +3 \quad +3 \quad +3$$
$$2, \; 5, \; 8, \; 11, \; 14$$

perimeter the distance around a figure (Lessons 27, 30)

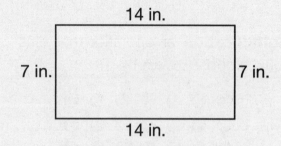

14 in.

7 in.

7 in.

14 in.

$$7 + 14 + 7 + 14 = 42$$

The perimeter is 42 inches.

picture graph a graph that uses symbols or pictures to show data (Lesson 24)

Balloon Colors Used

Red	⬭ ⬭ ⬭
Blue	⬭ ⬭ ⬭ ⬭ ⬭ ⬭
Green	⬭ ⬭ ⬭ ⬭

Key: Each ⬭ = 2 balloons

place value the value of a digit based on its position in a number (Lesson 10)

Thousands	Hundreds	Tens	Ones
1,	3	4	8

polygon a closed figure with three or more line segments as sides (Lesson 31)

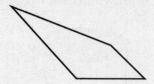

product the result of multiplying two or more numbers (Lessons 1, 3, 5)

$$8 \times 2 = 16$$
↑
product

quadrilateral a polygon with four sides and four angles (Lesson 31)

quotient the result of a division problem (Lessons 2, 4, 5)

$$36 \div 9 = 4$$
↑
quotient

rectangle a quadrilateral with 4 right angles and opposite sides that are parallel and the same length (Lessons 29, 31)

regroup to replace an amount with another amount of the same value (Lesson 13)

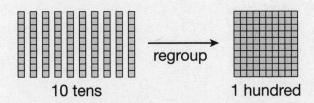

10 tens → 1 hundred

You can regroup 10 tens as 1 hundred.

rhombus a quadrilateral with opposite sides that are parallel and all 4 sides that are the same length (Lesson 31)

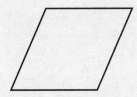

round to find a number close to a given number that tells about how many or about how much (Lessons 8, 11)

138 rounded to the nearest ten is 140.

138 rounded to the nearest hundred is 100.

rule tells how numbers in a pattern are related (Lesson 9)

8, 12, 16, 20, 24

The rule is add 4.

scale equally spaced numbers used as labels on a graph (Lesson 25)

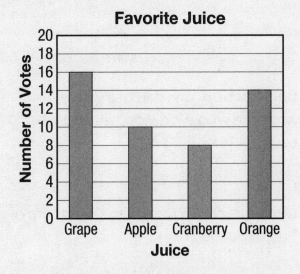

The graph has a scale of 2.

square a quadrilateral with 4 right angles and 4 sides that are the same length (Lesson 31)

standard form a way of writing numbers using the digits 0–9, with each digit having a place value (Lesson 10)

1,257 is written in standard form.

subtrahend the number being subtracted from another number (Lesson 14)

$16 - 9 = 7$
↑
subtrahend

sum the result of adding two or more numbers (Lesson 13)

$$5 + 3 = 8$$

↑
sum

unit fraction one part of a whole when the whole is divided into equal parts (Lessons 16, 32)

$$\frac{1}{2}, \frac{1}{3}, \frac{1}{4}, \cdots$$

unit square a square with side length of 1 unit (Lesson 28)

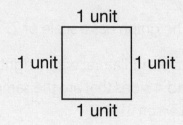

word form a way of writing numbers using words (Lesson 10)

215 in word form is two hundred fifteen.

Counters

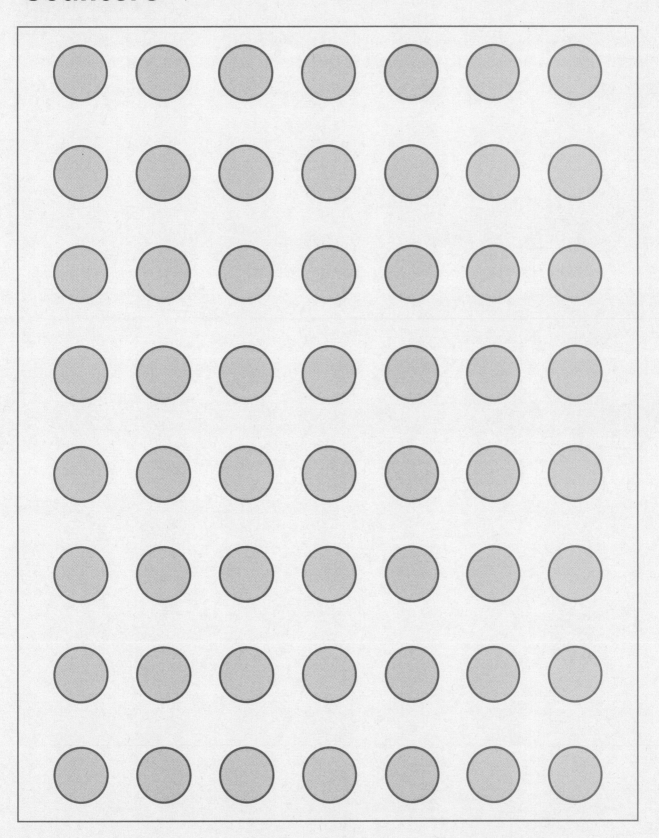

10 by 10 Grids

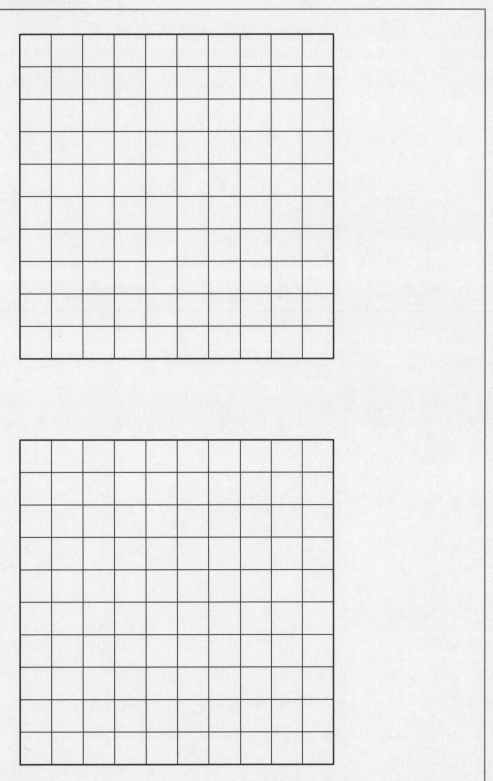

Tiles

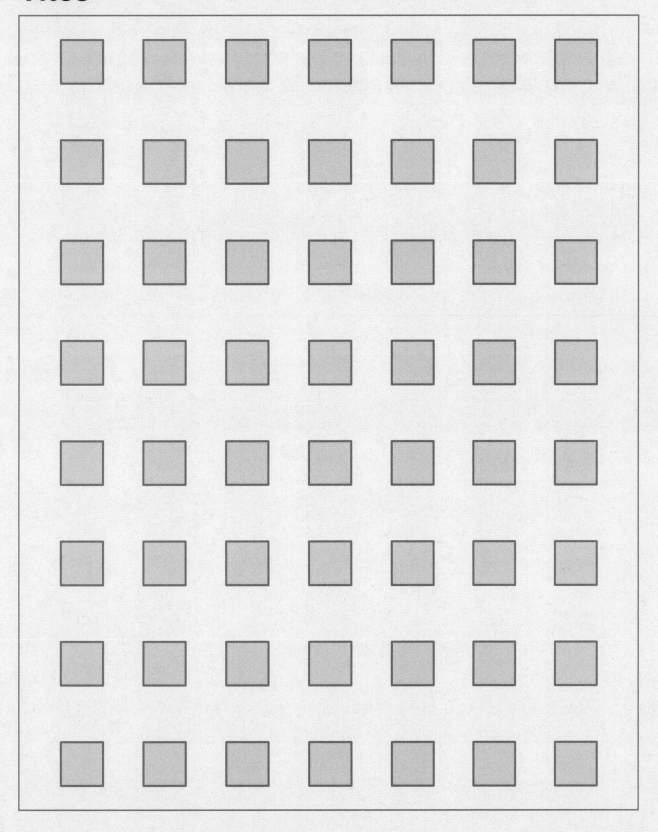

Multiplication Table

×	0	1	2	3	4	5	6	7	8	9	10
0	0	0	0	0	0	0	0	0	0	0	0
1	0	1	2	3	4	5	6	7	8	9	10
2	0	2	4	6	8	10	12	14	16	18	20
3	0	3	6	9	12	15	18	21	24	27	30
4	0	4	8	12	16	20	24	28	32	36	40
5	0	5	10	15	20	25	30	35	40	45	50
6	0	6	12	18	24	30	36	42	48	54	60
7	0	7	14	21	28	35	42	49	56	63	70
8	0	8	16	24	32	40	48	56	64	72	80
9	0	9	18	27	36	45	54	63	72	81	90
10	0	10	20	30	40	50	60	70	80	90	100

Multiplication Properties

Associative Property of Multiplication

The grouping of the factors does not change the product.

$(2 \times 5) \times 4 = 2 \times (5 \times 4)$

$10 \times 4 = 2 \times 20$

$40 = 40$

$(1 \times 5) \times 6 = 1 \times (5 \times 6)$

$5 \times 6 = 1 \times 30$

$30 = 30$

Commutative Property of Multiplication

The order of the factors does not change the product.

$5 \times 6 = 6 \times 5$

$30 = 30$

$4 \times 9 = 9 \times 4$

$36 = 36$

Identity Property of 1

Any number multiplied by 1 is that number.

$8 \times 1 = 8$

$1 \times 10 = 10$

Distributive Property of Multiplication

Multiplying the sum of two numbers by a factor is the same as multiplying each addend by the factor and adding the products.

$$8 \times 9 = 8 \times (5 + 4)$$
$$= (8 \times 5) + (8 \times 4)$$
$$= 40 + 32$$
$$= 72$$
$$8 \times 9 = 72$$

Blank Multiplication Table

×	0	1	2	3	4	5	6	7	8	9	10
0											
1											
2											
3											
4											
5											
6											
7											
8											
9											
10											

Addition Table

+	0	1	2	3	4	5	6	7	8	9	10
0	0	1	2	3	4	5	6	7	8	9	10
1	1	2	3	4	5	6	7	8	9	10	11
2	2	3	4	5	6	7	8	9	10	11	12
3	3	4	5	6	7	8	9	10	11	12	13
4	4	5	6	7	8	9	10	11	12	13	14
5	5	6	7	8	9	10	11	12	13	14	15
6	6	7	8	9	10	11	12	13	14	15	16
7	7	8	9	10	11	12	13	14	15	16	17
8	8	9	10	11	12	13	14	15	16	17	18
9	9	10	11	12	13	14	15	16	17	18	19
10	10	11	12	13	14	15	16	17	18	19	20

Place-Value Models

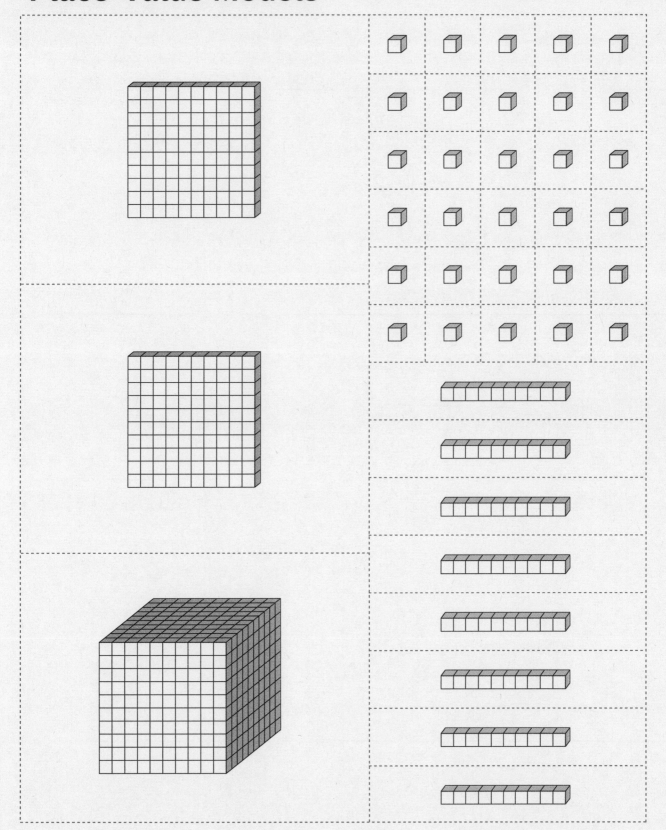

Place-Value Chart

Ten Thousands	Thousands	Hundreds	Tens	Ones

Ten Thousands	Thousands	Hundreds	Tens	Ones

Ten Thousands	Thousands	Hundreds	Tens	Ones

Number Lines

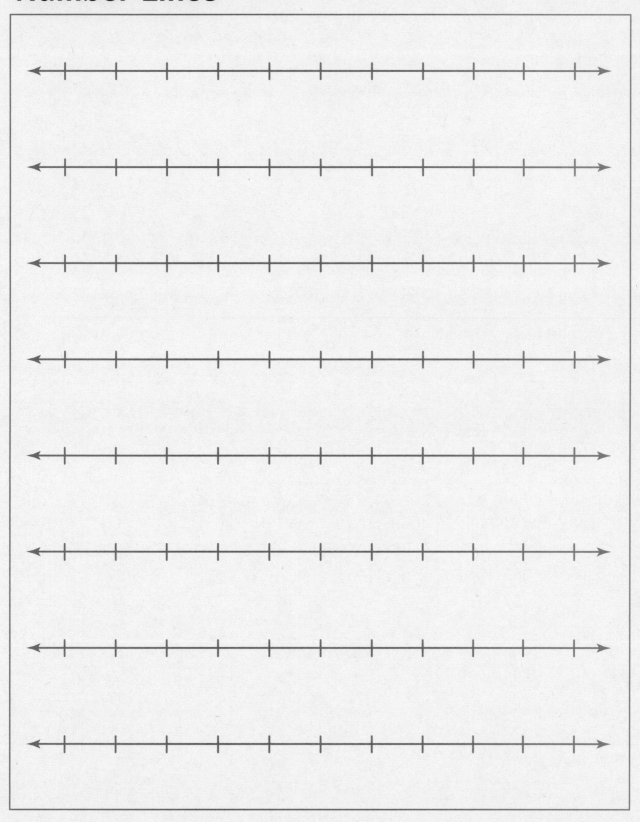

Addition Properties

Commutative Property of Addition

The order of the addends does not change the sum.

$$8 + 3 = 3 + 8$$
$$11 = 11$$

$$5 + 7 = 7 + 5$$
$$12 = 12$$

Associative Property of Addition

The grouping of the addends does not change the sum.

$$(7 + 8) + 2 = 7 + (8 + 2)$$
$$15 + 2 = 7 + 10$$
$$17 = 17$$

$$(8 + 5) + 5 = 8 + (5 + 5)$$
$$13 + 5 = 8 + 10$$
$$18 = 18$$

Identity Property of 0

The sum of any number and 0 is that number.

$$7 + 0 = 7$$

$$23 + 0 = 23$$

Distributive Property

Multiplying the sum of two numbers by a factor is the same as multiplying each addend by the factor and adding the products.

$$6 \times (5 + 2) = (6 \times 5) + (6 \times 2)$$
$$6 \times 7 = 30 + 12$$
$$42 = 42$$

Place-Value Mat

Hundreds

Tens

Ones

Addition and Subtraction Frames

H	T	O

+

H	T	O

+

H	T	O

−

H	T	O

−

Rectangular Grid

Fraction Models (Circles)

Fraction Models

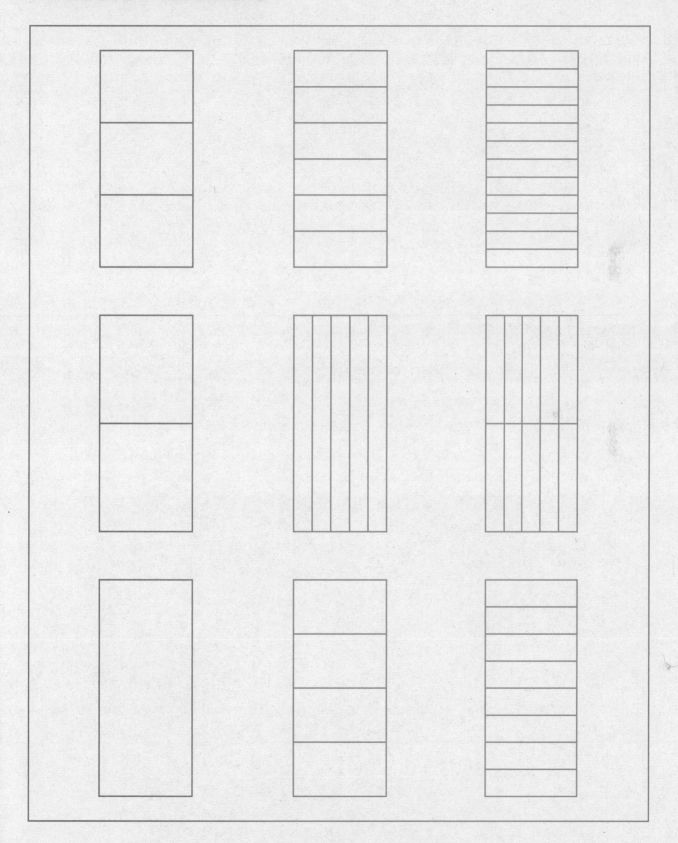

Fraction Strips

1

$\dfrac{1}{2}$	$\dfrac{1}{2}$

$\dfrac{1}{3}$	$\dfrac{1}{3}$	$\dfrac{1}{3}$

$\dfrac{1}{4}$	$\dfrac{1}{4}$	$\dfrac{1}{4}$	$\dfrac{1}{4}$

$\dfrac{1}{6}$	$\dfrac{1}{6}$	$\dfrac{1}{6}$	$\dfrac{1}{6}$	$\dfrac{1}{6}$	$\dfrac{1}{6}$

$\dfrac{1}{8}$	$\dfrac{1}{8}$	$\dfrac{1}{8}$	$\dfrac{1}{8}$	$\dfrac{1}{8}$	$\dfrac{1}{8}$	$\dfrac{1}{8}$	$\dfrac{1}{8}$

Clocks

Beakers

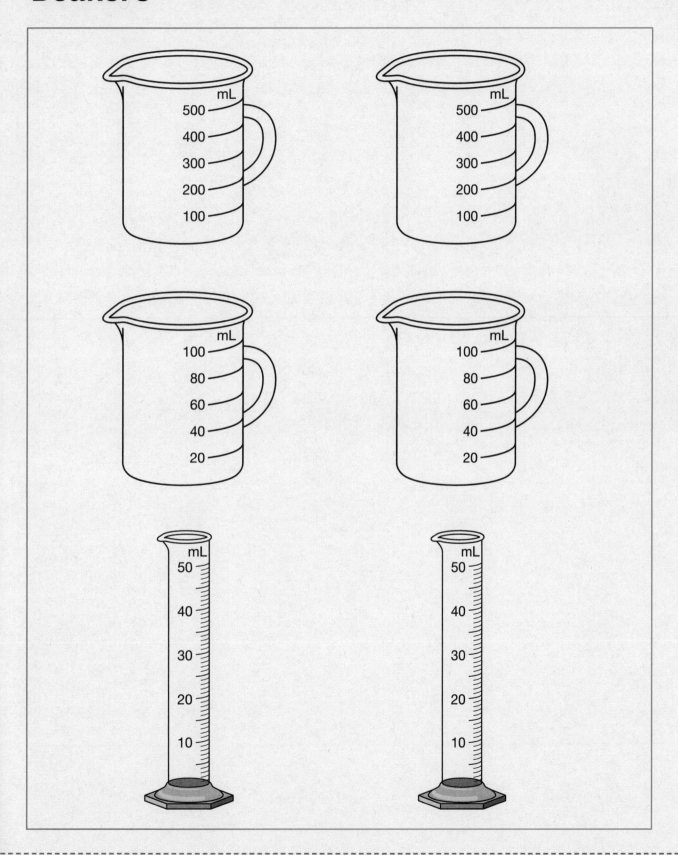

Two-Dimensional Figures

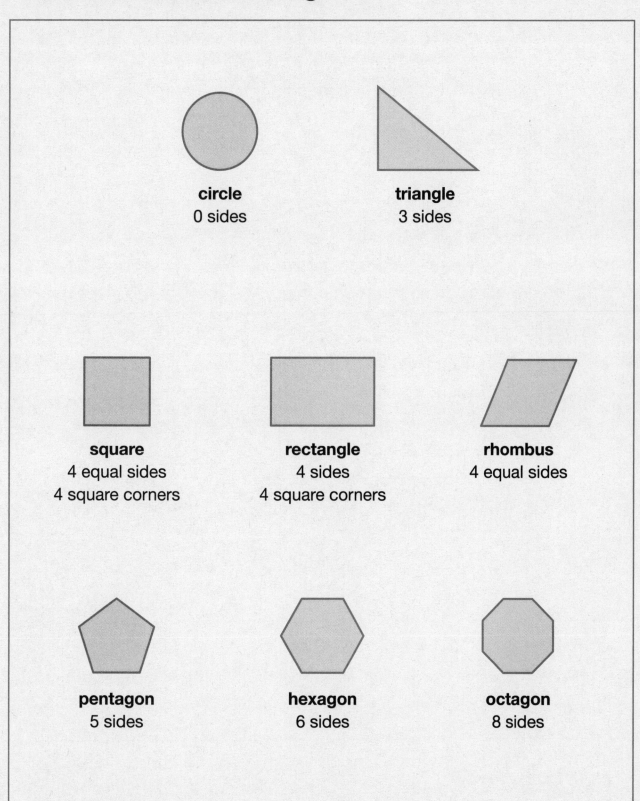

circle
0 sides

triangle
3 sides

square
4 equal sides
4 square corners

rectangle
4 sides
4 square corners

rhombus
4 equal sides

pentagon
5 sides

hexagon
6 sides

octagon
8 sides

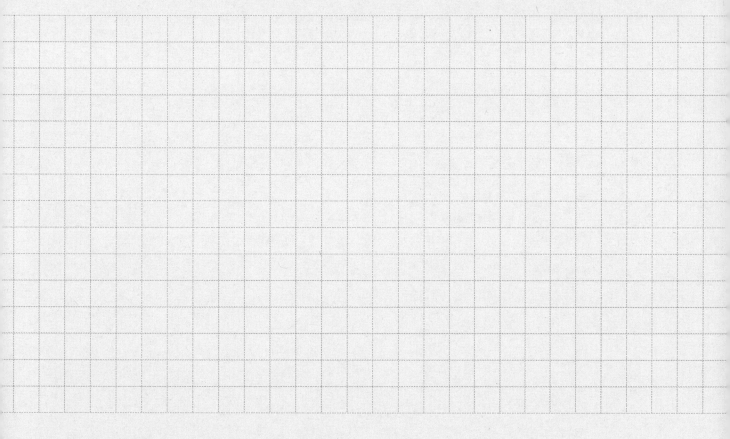

NOTES

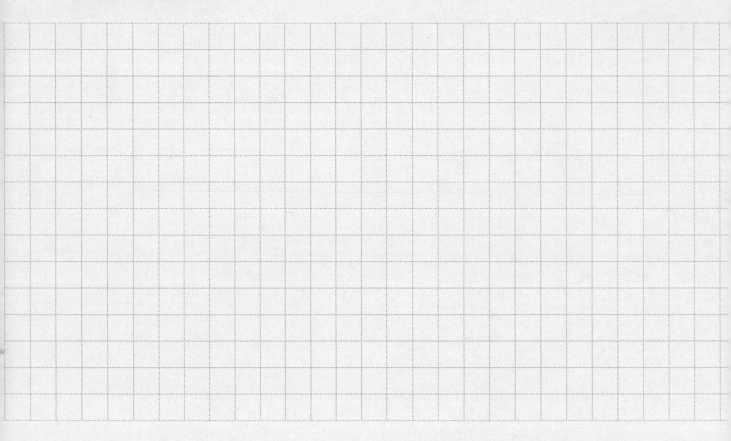